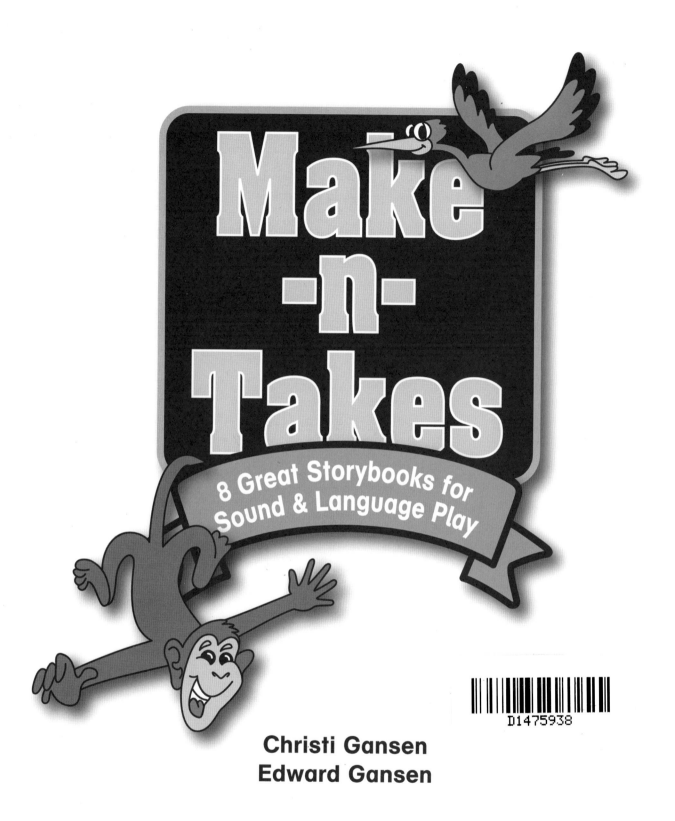

Make -n- Takes

8 Great Storybooks for Sound & Language Play

Christi Gansen
Edward Gansen

D1475938

Super Duper® Publications • Greenville, South Carolina

10 09 08 07 06 05 04   8 7 6 5 4 3 2

Library of Congress Cataloging-in-Publication Data

Gansen, Christi, date
   Make-n-Takes: 8 great storybooks for sound & language play / Christi Gansen and Edward Gansen ; [illustrations by Edward Gansen].
      p. cm.
   Includes bibliographical references.
   ISBN 1-932054-07-3 (pbk.)
   1. Reading—Phonetic method. 2. Reading (Early childhood)—Activity programs.
  I. Gansen, Edward, date II. Title.

LB1573.3.G36 2003
372.46'5—dc21
                          2003040278

Printed in China

Illustrations by Edward Gansen
Cover design by Debbie Olson

Trademarks: All brand names and product names used in this book are tradenames,
     service marks, trademarks, or registered trademarks of their respective owners.

www.superduperinc.com
P.O. Box 24997 • Greenville, SC 29616-2497 USA
1.800.277.8737 • Fax 1.800.978.7379

For Chloe and Cady,
who help us remember that being a kid should be fun.

About the Authors

Christi Gansen is a speech-language pathologist with the Edgerton School District in Edgerton, Wisconsin, where she has worked with preschool and early elementary students for the past 14 years. She holds a Master of Arts degree in Communication Disorders from the University of Northern Iowa and the Certificate of Clinical Competence in Speech-Language Pathology from the American Speech-Language-Hearing Association.

Edward Gansen is a freelance graphic designer and illustrator. He holds a Master of Arts degree in Advertising Design from Syracuse University.

Contents

Preface

Make-n-Takes for Phonology and Literacy developed from my desire for materials that would facilitate expressive phonology skills, provide children with engaging literacy experiences, and be time-efficient. Many of the children on my speech-language caseload needed intense phonological training, as well as language intervention. Finding the time in their schedule to do both separately and consistently was always a challenge. Incorporating stories into phonology training addressed this need, but it was difficult to find engaging stories that would facilitate production of target sounds. Some intervention materials were available with stories written to target specific sounds or phonological patterns, but the stories were often short and did not seem to offer much utility for language or literacy development. Other resources identified popular children's books that contained specific sounds, but it was difficult to determine if sound patterns would occur frequently enough in the stories for them to be worthwhile for intervention. Again, time was an issue—time to find the specific book, time to determine frequency of occurrence of target sounds, time to become familiar with the story line, and time to devise activities related to the story that would reinforce target sound productions.

Ed and I initially set out to write and illustrate three stories that would target final /s/ clusters. We were inspired by our own love of Dr. Seuss to use rhyming and fanciful story lines we hoped would engage both young listeners and the adults who would be reading and working with them. Discussions with Linda Schreiber at Thinking Publications prompted the expansion of the series to include the primary phonological targets recommended by Hodson, Scherz, and Strattman (2002). As the story lines developed, it seemed natural to link other language and literacy activities to the themes so that they could be used by more than just speech-language pathologists for intervention. In its final form, *Make-n-Takes* provides clinicians and teachers with a time-efficient and fun way to promote sound and sound pattern acquisition, early literacy, and language skills.

Acknowledgments

Our deepest appreciation goes to the many people who have inspired and supported us in the development of these materials. Special thanks go to Christi's colleagues in the Edgerton School District, who offer endless encouragement and are always open to new ideas, especially Judy Heil, Suzanne Granger, and Sharee Witt, for trying early versions of *Make-n-Takes* with students and sharing feedback as we developed the materials. We want to thank the students and staff of Edgerton Community Elementary School in Edgerton, Wisconsin, and Adams Elementary School in Janesville, Wisconsin, for being enthusiastic audiences to early versions of our stories. We also appreciate the enthusiasm and efforts of the staff at Thinking Publications—Linda Schreiber, Joyce Olson, Debbie Olson, and Sarah Thurs. Finally, we wish to thank Rae Cuda, Linda Fitzgerald, Janet McCauley, and Jackie Reeder for their time and efforts reviewing *Make-n-Takes* in its final stages.

Introduction

Overview

Make-n-Takes for Phonology and Lieracy is the first release in the *Make-n-Takes* series, especially designed to target the primary sound patterns in the cycles phonological remediation approach (Hodson, 1997, 2000; Hodson, Scherz, and Strattman, 2002). *Make-n-Takes* contains eight stories that target the following patterns for ages 3–9 years:

- Initial anteriors (/t, d, n/)
- Initial and final /s/ clusters (/sm, sn, sp, st, sk, ps, ts, ks/)
- Liquids (/l/ and /l/ clusters and /r/ and /r/ clusters)

The eight stories in the companion resource book, *More Make-n-Takes* (Gansen and Gansen, 2003), target syllableness, prevocalic consonants, postvocalic consonants, and velars. Either resource book in the series may be used separately, or both may be used to target all primary target patterns. Each of the eight units in each resource book contains a list of the words and speech sounds targeted in the storybook, so users may individualize their story selection based on the needs of each child.

The units contain all the needed materials: the storybook, sequence cards, picture cards, word count lists, picture card lists, production practice and carryover activities, and extension activities. Appendix A provides a summary of the target phonemes and patterns in each story, as well as other language skills that may be targeted in intervention. Black-and-white storybooks, sequence cards, and picture cards may be photocopied from this book (pages are perforated for easy removal, if desired) or they may be printed from the accompanying CD-ROM: *Make-n-Takes Software Companion*. Full-color versions of the storybooks and sequence cards may also be printed from the CD-ROM. Instructions for creating full-size and child-size storybooks are contained in Appendix B and in the Table of Contents file on the CD-ROM.

Target Audience

The *Make-n-Takes* series is appropriate for children from 3 to 9 years of age. The materials may be used by speech-language pathologists to facilitate speech production using a phonological process approach or traditional articulation remediation. The materials may also be used by general and special educators to develop receptive and expressive language, cognitive concepts, and early literacy skills, including phonological awareness and concepts of print.

Goals

Make-n-Takes for Phonology and Lieracy supports the development of children's expressive and receptive language and early literacy skills. Each unit may be used to target these goals:

- Increase speech intelligibility
- Increase perception and production of target phonological patterns or speech sounds
- Use target language features in the context of a story (See Appendix A for a list of possible language targets.)
- Increase early literacy skills, including phonological awareness and concepts of print

Background

According to Hodson and Paden (1991), a vital component of phonological remediation is providing opportunities to practice sound patterns in controlled activities that are natural and meaningful to a child. Ideally, children with expressive phonological delays are identified during the preschool years, a time when it is also important for them to be exposed to numerous literacy experiences (Burns, Griffin, and Snow, 1999). Since reading stories is a common activity for preschool and school-aged children, incorporating stories in phonological sessions provides natural and meaningful contexts to hear and practice sound patterns and to begin building early literacy skills.

The concept of using story formats in phonological remediation is not new. Resources are available that identify which popular children's books contain specific sounds. Some include sound-specific word lists, but do not necessarily give an exact count of the number of times the words occur in the stories; others provide a total count of the words but do not delineate the count according to word position or blend combinations (e.g., final /ps/ or final /ks/). Without complete word count information, it is difficult to determine if sound patterns will occur frequently enough for the story to be worthwhile for phonological remediation. Some intervention materials have been written for specific phonemes or target patterns. While these stories have a high frequency of the target phonemes or patterns, their content is generally limited to a short story that has little application for literacy learning. The story lines themselves are not designed to readily lead children to acquire other academic or critical thinking skills.

Make-n-Takes: 8 Great Storybooks for Sound & Language Play was developed to merge the goals of phonological remediation with rich literary experiences. The stories incorporate a high concentration of words containing a target phonological pattern in progressive, rhyming story lines. The format provides opportunities for listening to (i.e., auditory bombardment) and speaking the target pattern while exposing children to another level of phonological awareness through rhyming. From an academic and literacy perspective, the stories facilitate sequencing, oral storytelling, narrative structure, critical thinking skills, and number concepts. Extension activities related to each story are provided to address these areas. Activities can be implemented in remediation sessions, the classroom, or at home. Clinicians can consult with teachers and parents regarding the goals of the remediation program and how to use activities or techniques that will facilitate carryover of learning to other settings.

Before You Begin...

Before beginning intervention, administer a formal articulation or phonological assessment, such as *The Assessment of Phonological Processes–Revised* (Hodson, 1986). This will provide baseline information for setting goals and measuring progress. Traditional articulation tests will identify specific phonemes to address, while a phonological process analysis will identify the child's error processes and the phonological patterns that need to be developed to increase intelligibility.

According to Hodson and Paden's (1991) approach, a phonological process analysis is used to measure the frequency of error processes before beginning intervention and again after each phonological cycle to measure progress. Children produce words during interactions with specific objects, and their productions are transcribed according to the types of phonological processes the child uses. Percentages of occurrence are computed for the various deviant processes, and a level of severity for phonological delays is determined. When a child is identified as having a significant phonological delay, Hodson et al. (2002) offer several suggestions for determining which patterns to target and in what order (see Figure 1). Intervention is structured in phonological cycles, during which each target phonological pattern is addressed in succession.

Analyze the assessment information and plan which phonological patterns to target in a cycle. Sixty minutes per target sound within a pattern is recommended. Once targets are identified, individual sessions can be planned.

Figure 1

Potential Target Patterns

Primary Potential Target Patterns

(For beginning cycles; target only those that are consistently deficient *and* stimulable.)

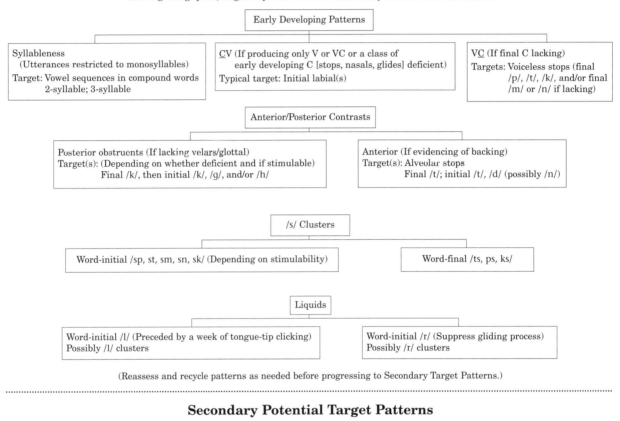

Early Developing Patterns

Syllableness
(Utterances restricted to monosyllables)
Target: Vowel sequences in compound words
2-syllable; 3-syllable

CV (If producing only V or VC or a class of early developing C [stops, nasals, glides] deficient)
Typical target: Initial labial(s)

VC (If final C lacking)
Targets: Voiceless stops (final /p/, /t/, /k/, and/or final /m/ or /n/ if lacking)

Anterior/Posterior Contrasts

Posterior obstruents (If lacking velars/glottal)
Target(s): (Depending on whether deficient and if stimulable)
Final /k/, then initial /k/, /g/, and/or /h/

Anterior (If evidencing of backing)
Target(s): Alveolar stops
Final /t/; initial /t/, /d/ (possibly /n/)

/s/ Clusters

Word-initial /sp, st, sm, sn, sk/ (Depending on stimulability)

Word-final /ts, ps, ks/

Liquids

Word-initial /l/ (Preceded by a week of tongue-tip clicking)
Possibly /l/ clusters

Word-initial /r/ (Suppress gliding process)
Possibly /r/ clusters

(Reassess and recycle patterns as needed before progressing to Secondary Target Patterns.)

Secondary Potential Target Patterns

(After establishment of early developing patterns, contrastive use of velars/alveolars, /s/ cluster emergence in conversation, and suppression of gliding while producing liquids in carefully selected production-practice words, progress to secondary patterns that remain problematic; incorporate minimal pairs whenever possible.)

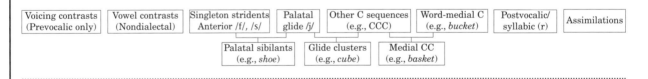

Voicing contrasts (Prevocalic only)

Vowel contrasts (Nondialectal)

Singleton stridents Anterior /f/, /s/

Palatal glide /j/

Other C sequences (e.g., CCC)

Word-medial C (e.g., *bucket*)

Postvocalic/ syllabic (r)

Assimilations

Palatal sibilants (e.g., *shoe*)

Glide clusters (e.g., *cube*)

Medial CC (e.g., *basket*)

Advanced Potential Target Patterns

(For upper-elementary-grade-level children with intelligibility problems.)

Complex consonant sequences (e.g., *extra*)

Multisyllabicity (e.g., *unanimous*)

Using *Make-n-Takes* for Phonological Remediation

Overview of Materials

Each of the eight units in this resource book includes a black-and-white storybook, corresponding sequence cards, picture cards (i.e., reproducible black-and-white line drawings of target words), a list of words from the story that use the target pattern with frequency of occurrence counts and totals, a list of items depicted on the picture cards, a list of activities for production practice and carryover outside of intervention, and suggested extension activities. Appendix A summarizes the target patterns and language skills emphasized in each storybook. The CD-ROM contains black-and-white and color versions of the storybooks in two sizes, black-and-white and color versions of the sequence cards, and black-and-white picture cards—all in Portable Document Format (PDF) for printing.

Session Overview

Phonological sessions begin with a short period of auditory bombardment targeting the sound pattern for that session. Children listen carefully while the clinician reads or says aloud a list of 10–15 single words (from the word count list[s] for the story) that contain the target pattern. Slight amplification using binaural amplifiers is recommended. Small amplifiers, headsets, and connectors are available for a nominal cost at electronic supply stores (e.g., RadioShack). Visual and tactile cues should be used to emphasize the target pattern.

Next, children create their own picture cards for stimulable target words (usually three to five pictures per session). The story's picture cards can be photocopied from the corresponding unit or printed from the CD-ROM ahead of time for children to color, or children can draw their own pictures to color. Target words can be elicited during this step by requiring children to ask for the picture cards they want to color next or by having them tell what they have colored when they are finished. More intense production practice is then conducted by incorporating the picture cards and target words into structured play or learning activities (usually two or three per session). Sessions conclude with another short period of auditory bombardment. Stimulability probing for the next session's target words can be conducted at the end of the session as well. The following sections describe how to use the materials within a session.

Storybooks

Use one or more of these activities to incorporate the storybook into a phonological remediation session:

- Photocopy the black-and-white story pages from the chosen unit, or print the black-and-white storybooks from the *Make-n-Takes Software Companion*. Or, using a color inkjet or color laser printer connected to your computer or network, print the color storybooks from the accompanying CD-ROM. All stories may be printed as either full-size (11" wide by 8½" high) or child-size (5½" wide by 4¼" high). Directions for assembling the storybooks may be found in Appendix B or in the Table of Contents file on the CD-ROM. Use the storybooks for clinician-directed activities.

- Read the storybook aloud to children to model the target sound and to provide meaningful contexts to use the practice words.

- As children become familiar with the story line and the pictures, let them finish lines with target words or repeat words that you say.

- While reading, ask questions that require children to use target words to answer.

- For younger children or children with shorter attention spans, break the stories into shorter segments to read during each session or have the children act out the stories as they are read.

- Target question comprehension skills by asking questions about the story as you read it or by asking questions at the end of the story.

- Model and encourage predicting and problem solving as stories unfold.

- Reinforce number concepts by counting objects in the illustrations and pointing out examples of one-to-one correspondence.

- Print and assemble the child-size black-and-white storybook from the *Make-n-Takes Software Companion*, following the instructions in Appendix B. Make a personal book for each child.

- Have children color the target words on the pages of their personal child-size storybook.

- Send the personal child-size storybooks home with suggestions for home activities.

Refer to the Production Practice and Carryover Activities in each unit for additional ideas.

Sequence Cards

Use these language development activities to improve comprehension, sequencing, story structure, and memory skills:

- Tell the story using the sequence cards. Encourage children to help tell the story using target words.

- Have children recall events and sequence the pictures according to the story.

- Give simple directions to have children create new sequences with the pictures.

- Adjust the number of pictures to use in the sequence according to the child's ability and age.

- Allow children to create their own sequences and explain them to you using the same terms.

- Model and prompt use of the terms *first, second, next,* and *last* to tell the sequence.

- Use the sequence cards for visual memory tasks. Present a series of cards, then have children close their eyes while you remove one of the pictures. Have children tell which picture is missing.

- Target question comprehension skills and number concepts using single cards.

Picture Cards

Use these activities to individualize sessions:

- Determine stimulability by having children imitate potential target words you model. Use visual and tactile cues to help elicit target sounds. Avoid words with phonetic environments that may interfere with correct production of the target sound because of assimilation. For example, if a child is substituting /t/ for /k/, the use of target words that also contain /t/ (e.g., *cat* or *kit*) is likely to hinder correct production of the /k/ sound because of assimilation.

- Once each child's stimulable words are identified, photocopy the appropriate pictures to make individual picture cards.

- Children can help cut, color, and glue the pictures onto index cards and then use them for a variety of activities designed to elicit correct productions. The majority of the pictures are directly related to the story; however, there are some unrelated words that can be used for production practice and incorporated into activities that tie into the story.

- Use picture cards for new activities. For example, use a child's individual practice cards from *Our Parade with Two Blue Bikes* to create a new parade.

Word Count Lists

Use the Word Count Lists for these remediation and home activities:

- Use the corresponding word list(s) for each story to make individualized auditory bombardment lists for remediation sessions. Select 10–15 words from the list(s) and read them aloud at the beginning and end of each session. It is generally better to select words that are not being used for production practice, since children are asked to only listen to these words. (Oftentimes when a child hears a word that he or she has been asked to practice saying, it is difficult for the child to refrain from saying it during the listening time. The listening task is confused with the production task.) Ideally, children listen with headsets to receive amplification while the speech-language pathologist speaks into a microphone. If amplification is not available, the words are still read aloud.

- Send a copy of the word count list home when beginning a new target. Encourage caregivers to read the list aloud to their child daily (ideally two times per day) to facilitate awareness of the target pattern and to promote carryover to different settings. Remind caregivers that their child is only to listen to the words on the word list, not try to repeat them.

Picture Card Lists

Use the picture card list(s) as a reference for the picture cards available in each unit. The list(s) may also be used to generate a word list for auditory bombardment.

Production Practice and Carryover Activities

Use these suggestions to enhance the effectiveness of phonological remediation:

- Select activities from this list of ideas to elicit target sounds or patterns for each story. Activities are related to the theme or target words of the stories. They include use of both real objects and picture cards.

- Use these activities for production practice during remediation sessions.

- Send activities home for carryover practice.

Extension Activities

Use these suggested activities for all children who will benefit from language remediation or enrichment in a variety of settings:

- Use these ideas to facilitate a variety of language and literacy skills, including rhyming, vocabulary, semantics, syntax and morphology, sequencing, and critical thinking.

- Speech-language pathologists can monitor and reinforce sound production skills during breaks in phonological cycles while using the materials to address a variety of language skills.

- Classroom teachers can use the storybooks and sequence cards in the classroom setting to address concepts that all children need to develop (e.g., rhyming, sequencing, or storytelling) and at the same time provide a natural setting for identified children to transfer their phonological skills.

- Use Appendix A to find skills addressed by extension activities for each story.

The Role of Caregivers

Involvement from caregivers plays an important role in the success of any child's learning. Ongoing consultation and communication with caregivers is vital for them to understand the goals of the program and the techniques they can use at home to facilitate carryover of learning to natural settings. *Make-n-Takes* includes a variety of practice and extension activities that can be shared with caregivers.

- During phonological intervention, send home corresponding auditory bombardment lists to be read daily. These lists contain a variety of words that use the target pattern. Remind parents that the child should only listen to the words and repeat them.

- Select picture cards that the child produces correctly and send them home after each session, along with suggestions for how to use the cards in play activities. Explain to caregivers the visual and tactile cues they can use to help elicit the target sound from their child.

Measuring Progress

Measure phonological progress formally by readministering an assessment tool such as *The Assessment of Phonological Processes–Revised* (Hodson, 1986) at the end of a cycle. During sessions, make anecdotal notes describing individual children's productions, the types of cues they require, and environments where they are successful with productions (e.g., small-group setting, classroom, or home) to keep track of progress and carryover that may be occurring. For traditional articulation intervention, chart and collect data of correct and incorrect productions.

Appendices

Summary of Target Patterns and Extension Activity Skills

		Diving Down Deep in Our New Submarine	The King of the Forest	Strange Stuff We Spot on Our Way to School	The Brown Pups Are Missing	What's in the Big Closet?	Our Parade with Two Blue Bikes	Leapin' Lizards' Big Zoo Hullabaloo	Train, Truck, and Tractor
Target Patterns									
Initial Anteriors	/t/	•							
	/d/	•							
	/n/	•							
Initial /s/ Clusters	/sm/		•						
	/sn/		•						
	/sp/			•					
	/st/			•					
	/sk/			•					
Final /s/ Clusters	/ps/				•				
	/ts/					•			
	/ks/						•		
Initial Liquids	/l/							•	
	/l/ clusters							•	
	/r/								•
	/r/ clusters								•
Extension Activity Skills									
Rhyming		•	•	•	•	•	•	•	•
Vocabulary Development		•	•	•	•	•	•	•	•
Synonyms			•		•				
Attributes								•	
Associations				•		•			
Functions				•		•			
Multiple-Meaning Words					•				
Absurdities		•					•		
Classification		•						•	•
Plurals					•	•	•	•	
Possessives				•				•	
Present Progressive Verbs		•							
Past Tense Verbs			•						
Comparatives/Superlatives									•
Sequencing		•			•		•		
Critical Thinking		•	•	•	•	•	•	•	•

How to Create a Full-Size Black-and-White Storybook

What You'll Need

- Adobe Acrobat Reader® (If you don't already have Acrobat Reader installed on your computer, you must first install the program to your hard drive. You can download a free copy from http://www.adobe.com.

- A photocopier, or an inkjet or laser printer connected to your computer or computer network (To avoid ink bleedthrough, you may want to use heavy-stock paper.)

- A comb- or spiral-binding system or other fasteners (If you'd rather not bind the book yourself, print shops, photocopy shops, and office-supply stores [e.g., Office Max or Staples] offer affordable binding services. Check your local listings for availability.)

If you photocopy the pages from the book:

1. Tear out the storybook pages along the perforation. (If you choose not to remove the pages, the perforation helps the pages lie flat on the copy machine). Photocopy the pages from the book in a two-sided, landscape format. (Your page width should be 11" and page height 8½".)

2. (Before you bind the book together, it is recommended that you include a sheet of clear acetate over the front and back cover of the book or laminate them for durability and protection.) Collect the pages into the proper page sequence and secure with a fastener, such as a comb, spiral, or plastic binding, or metal or plastic rings. Trim the excess binding away, if necessary (see diagram on next page).

If you print the story from the CD-ROM:

1. Under File > Page Setup, select "Landscape" page orientation. (Your page width should be 11" and page height 8½".) Under File > Print, navigate to and select "Odd Pages Only." Print all odd-numbered pages, flip your printed stack over, and insert the printed pages in your printer's paper tray. Under File > Print, navigate to and select "Even Pages Only." Double-check your page orientation and page order to ensure that you print the

book properly as two-sided. (Alternatively, you may print all pages single-sided from your printer and use a duplexing photocopier to make the pages double-sided.)

2. (Before you bind the book together, it is recommended that you include a sheet of clear acetate over the front and back cover of the book or laminate them for durability and protection.) Collect the pages into the proper page sequence and secure with a fastener, such as a comb, spiral, or plastic binding, or metal or plastic rings. Trim the excess binding away, if necessary (see diagram below).

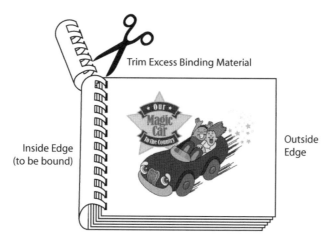

Binding your book as described in Step 2 allows for the largest possible viewing format, suitable for reading to a class or small group. When you're finished, a typical page spread in each book should resemble the diagram below.

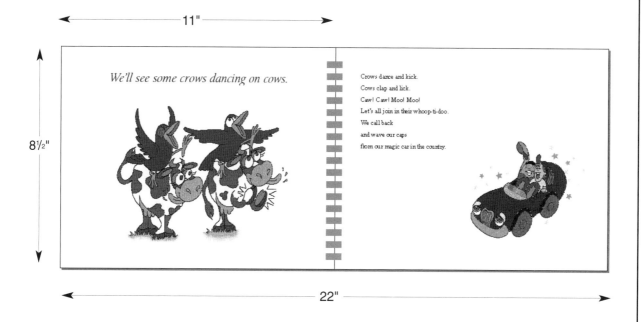

How to Create a Child-Size Black-and-White Storybook

What You'll Need

- Adobe Acrobat Reader® (If you don't already have Acrobat Reader installed on your computer, you must first install the program to your hard drive. You can download a free copy from http://www.adobe.com.

- A photocopier, or an inkjet or laser printer connected to your computer or computer network (To avoid ink bleedthrough, you may wish to use heavy-stock paper.)

- A stapler or other fasteners and glue or tape

1. Under File > Page Setup, select "Landscape" page orientation. (Your page width should be 11" and page height 8½".) Under File > Print, navigate to and select "Odd Pages Only." Print all odd-numbered pages, flip your printed stack over, and insert the printed pages in your printer's paper tray. Under File > Print, navigate to and select "Even Pages Only." Double-check your page orientation and page order to ensure that you print the book properly as two-sided. (Alternatively, you may print all pages single-sided from your printer and use a duplexing photocopier to make the pages double-sided.)

2. Trim then fold each page pair along the appropriate guidelines (see diagram below).

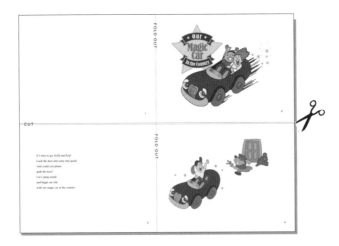

3. Collect the pages into the proper page sequence and secure along the left side with a stapler or other fastener, such as a comb, spiral, or plastic binding, or metal or plastic rings. Trim the excess binding away, if necessary (see diagram below). Depending on the length of the story, the center pages may be blank. Use glue or transparent tape along the edge of these pages to secure them together.

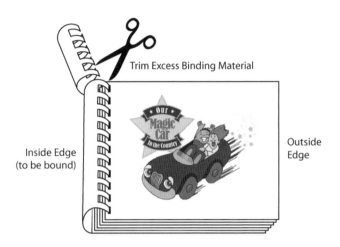

Trim Excess Binding Material

Inside Edge
(to be bound)

Outside
Edge

When you're finished, a typical page spread in each book should resemble the diagram below.

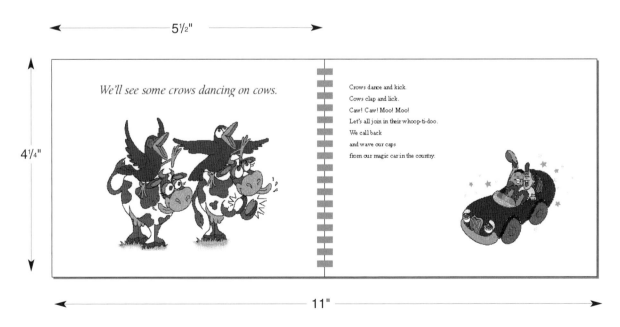

5½"

4¼"

11"

How to Create a Full-Size Color Storybook

What You'll Need

- Adobe Acrobat Reader® (If you don't already have Acrobat Reader installed on your computer, you must first install the program to your hard drive. You can download a free copy from http://www.adobe.com.

- A color inkjet or color laser printer connected to your computer or computer network (To avoid ink bleedthrough, you may wish to use heavy-stock paper.)

- Glue or double-stick tape

- A comb- or spiral-binding system or other fasteners (If you'd rather not bind the book yourself, print shops, photocopy shops, and office-supply stores [e.g., Office Max or Staples] offer affordable binding services. Check your local listings for availability.)

1. Under File > Page Setup, select "Landscape" page orientation. (Your page width should be 11" and page height 8½".) Under File > Print, navigate to and select "Odd Pages Only." Print all odd-numbered pages, flip your printed stack over, and insert the printed pages in your color printer's paper tray. Under File > Print, navigate to and select "Even Pages Only." Double-check your page orientation and page order to ensure that you print the book properly as two-sided. (Alternatively, you may print all pages single-sided from your color printer and then use glue or double-sided tape to seal the blank sides of the pages together.)

2. (Before you bind the book together, it is recommended that you include a sheet of clear acetate over the front and back cover of the book or laminate them for durability and protection.) Collect the pages into the proper page sequence and secure with a fastener, such as a comb, spiral, or plastic binding, or metal or plastic rings. Trim the excess binding away, if necessary (see diagram that follows).

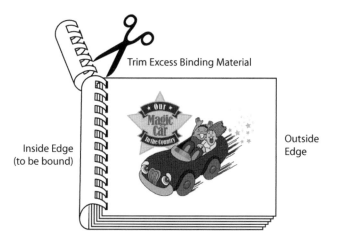

Binding your book as described in Step 2 allows for the largest possible viewing format, suitable for reading to a class or small group. When you're finished, a typical page spread in each book should resemble the diagram below.

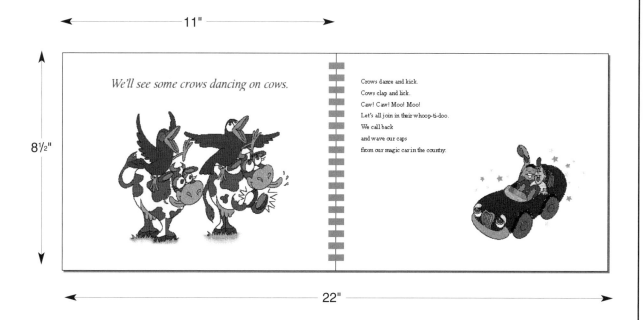

How to Create a Child-Size Color Storybook

What You'll Need

- Adobe Acrobat Reader® (If you don't already have Acrobat Reader installed on your computer, you must first install the program to your hard drive. You can download a free copy from http://www.adobe.com.

- A color inkjet or color laser printer connected to your computer or computer network (To avoid ink bleedthrough, you may wish to use heavy-stock paper.)

- A stapler or other fasteners and glue or tape

1. Under File > Page Setup, select "Landscape" page orientation. (Your page width should be 11" and page height 8½".) Under File > Print, navigate to and select "Odd Pages Only." Print all odd-numbered pages, flip your printed stack over, and insert the printed pages in your color printer's paper tray. Under File > Print, navigate to and select "Even Pages Only." Double-check your page orientation and page order to ensure that you print the book properly as two-sided.

2. Trim and fold each page pair along the appropriate guidelines (see diagram below).

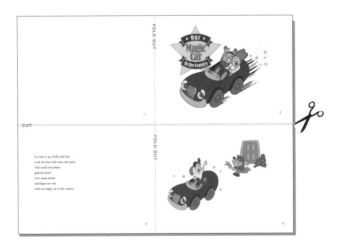

3. Collect the pages into the proper page sequence and secure along the left side with a stapler or other fastener, such as a comb, spiral, or plastic binding, or metal or plastic rings. Trim the excess binding away, if necessary (see diagram below). Depending on the length of the story, the center pages may be blank. Use glue or transparent tape along the edge of these pages to secure them together.

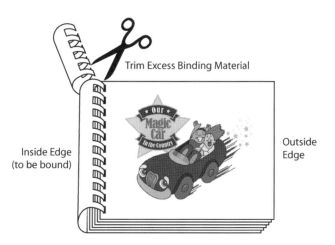

When you're finished, a typical page spread in each book should resemble the diagram below.

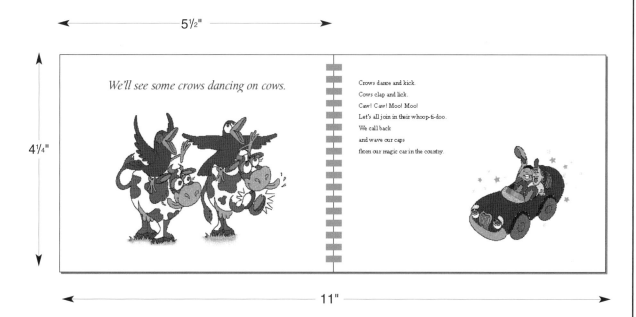

References

Burns, M.S., Griffin, P., and Snow, C. (Eds.). (1999). *Starting out right: A guide to promoting children's reading success.* Washington, DC: National Academy Press.

Gansen, C., and Gansen, E. (2003). *More make-n-takes.* Greenville, SC: Super Duper Publications.

Hodson, B. (1986). *The Assessment of Phonological Processes–Revised.* Austin, TX: Pro-Ed.

Hodson, B.W. (1997). Disordered phonologies: What have we learned about assessment and treatment? In B. Hodson and M. Edwards (Eds.), *Perspectives in applied phonology* (pp. 197–224). New York: Aspen.

Hodson, B.W. (2000, March). Enhancing phonological and metaphonological skills: What we know in the year 2000. Presentation at the annual convention of the Wisconsin Speech-Language-Hearing Association, Milwaukee, WI.

Hodson, B.W., and Paden, E.P. (1991). *Targeting intelligible speech: A phonological approach to remediation* (2nd ed.). Austin, TX: Pro-Ed.

Hodson, B.W., Scherz, J.A., and Strattman, K.H. (2002). Evaluating communicative abilities of a highly unintelligible preschooler. *American Journal of Speech-Language Pathology, 11,* 236–242.

The 8 Great
Storybook Units

Diving Down Deep
IN OUR
New
Submarine

Tick, tock,
at ten until two,
we're diving down deep
in the water so blue.

We're taking a tour
to terrific sea sights
in a new submarine,
complete with pink lights.

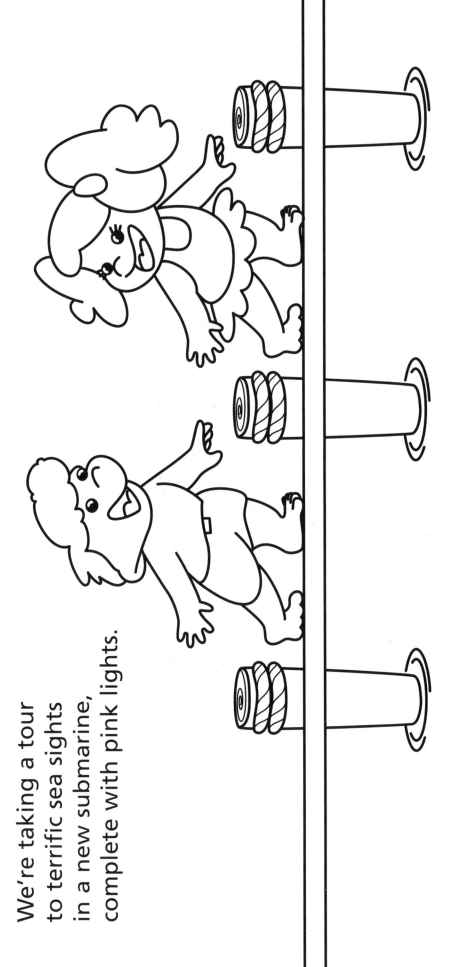

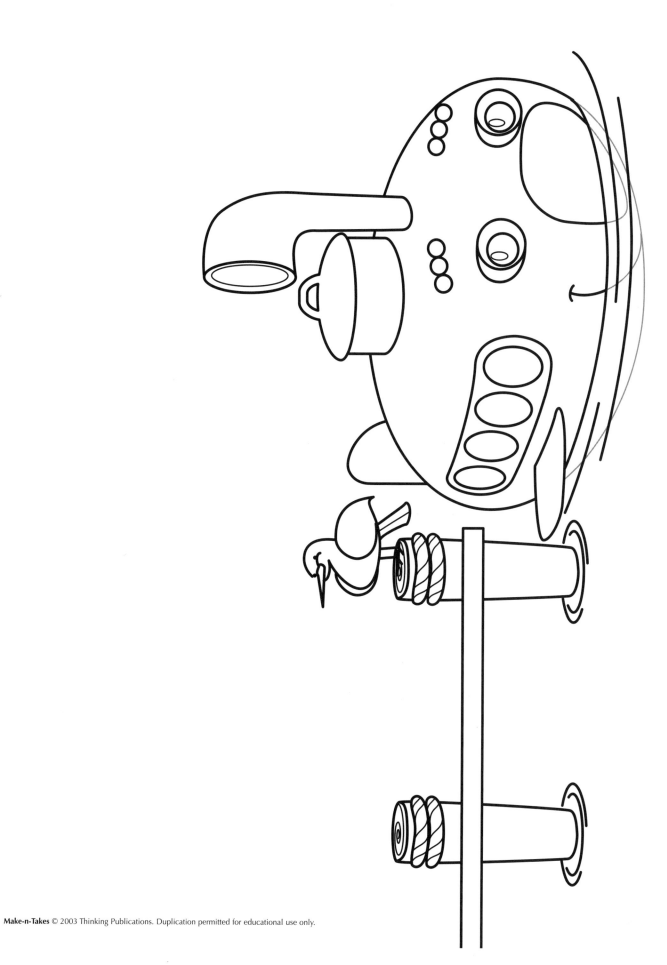

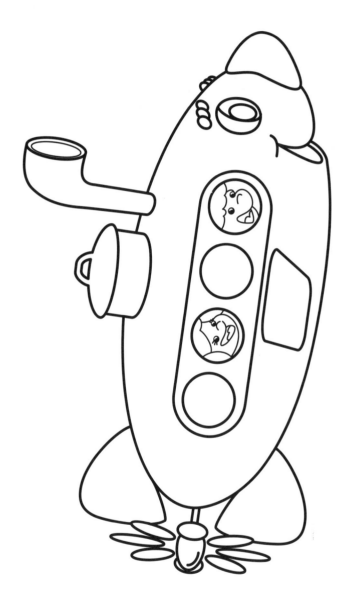

Tick, tock,
we're starting our trip.
First stop is a reef
with an old sunken ship.

The inside seems dark,
the outside all dirty.
We knock on the door
of a turtle named Gertie.

We stop in for tea
and nibble noodle cake.
It's nice to relax
and nap until eight.

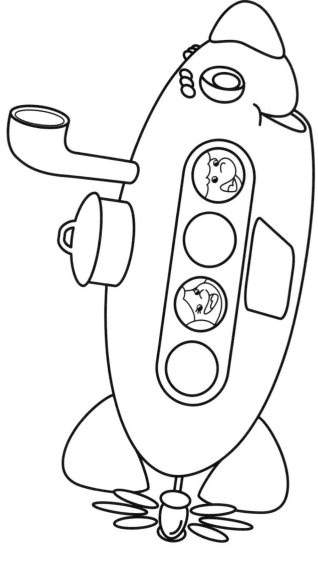

Tick, tock,
now we move on.
Time to see starfish
and a dolphin named Don.

Don and the starfish
perform nifty tricks,
balancing clams
on top of tall sticks.

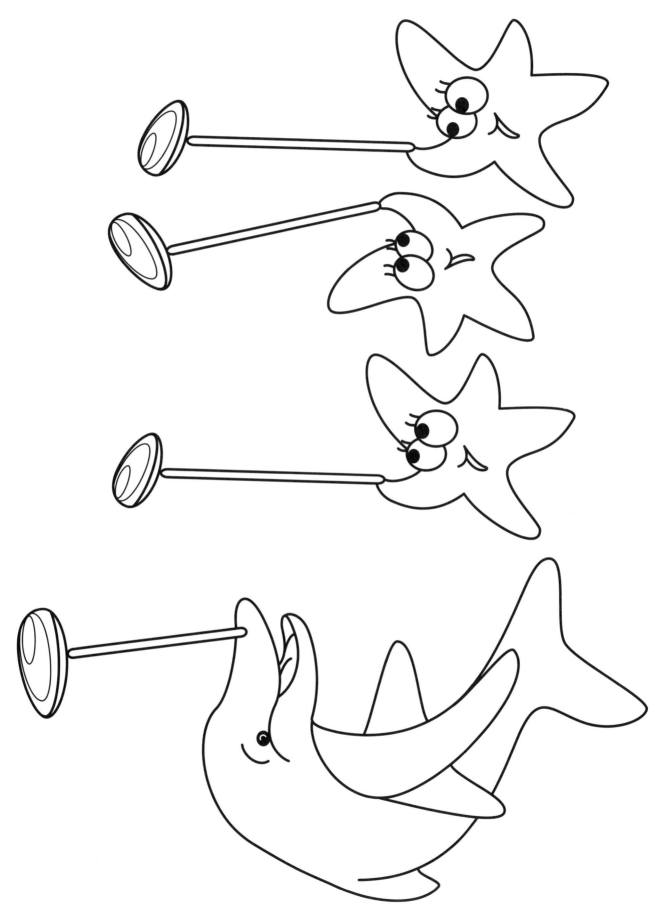

Tick, tock,
no time to be tardy.
Our new submarine
is off to a party
hosted by nine newts
(all are named Nellie!)
twirling their tails
and tickling our belly.

10

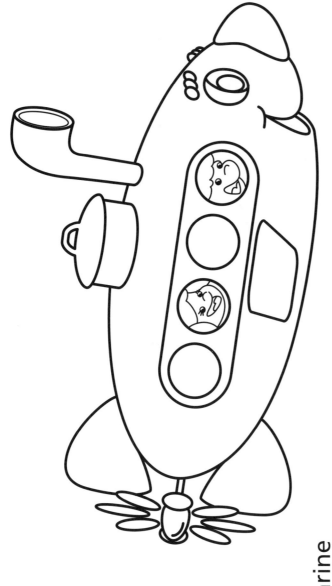

Tick, tock,
our new submarine
takes us down deep
to a new water scene.

An octopus cave
next to a mountain
dazzles our eyes
with a green neon fountain.

Dave the Old Octopus
is jamming out tunes.
Six arms toot trumpets,
the last two tap spoons!

Tick, tock,
we run out of time.
Our new submarine
is due back by nine.

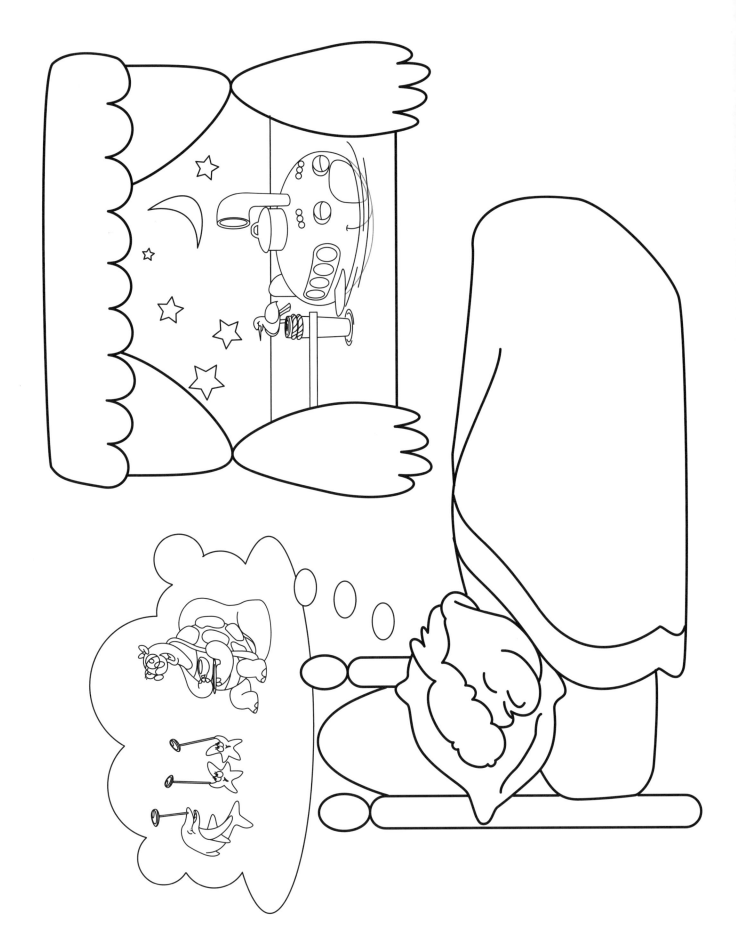

Back at the dock
we're tired and dead
from deep diving travel.
We're ready for bed!

All snug under covers,
we doze off and dream
of our undersea neighbors
and our new submarine!

Sequence Cards

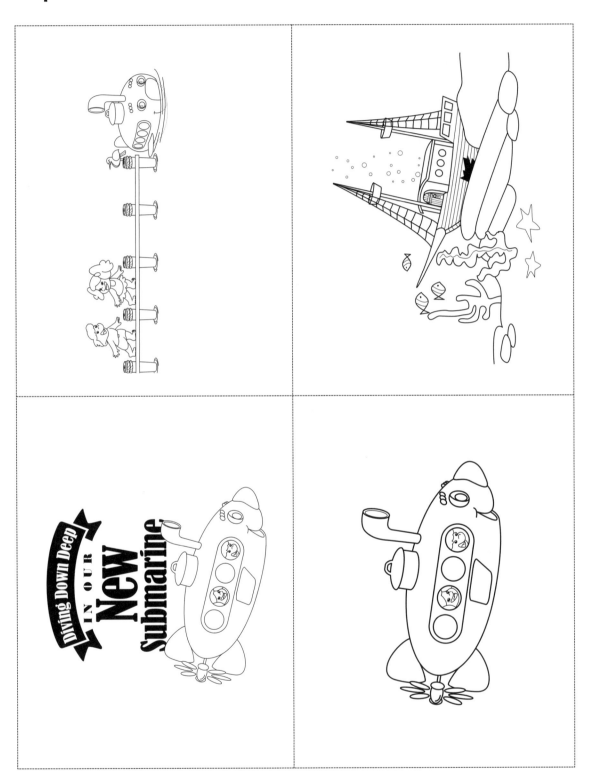

Sequence Cards

Sequence Cards

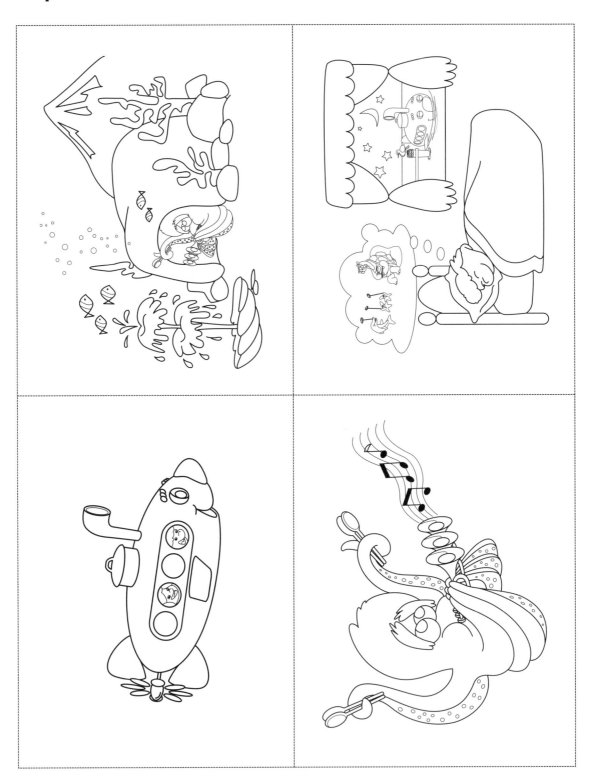

Picture Cards

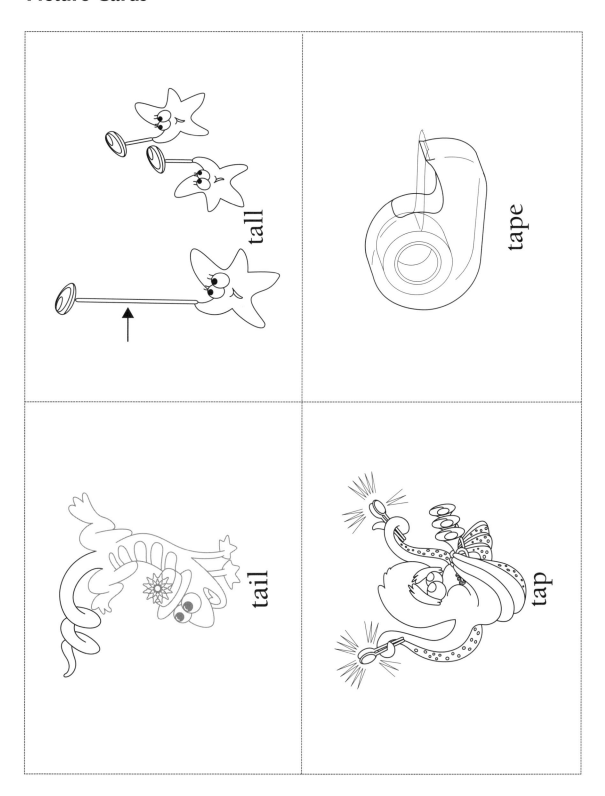

tail

tap

tail

tape

Picture Cards

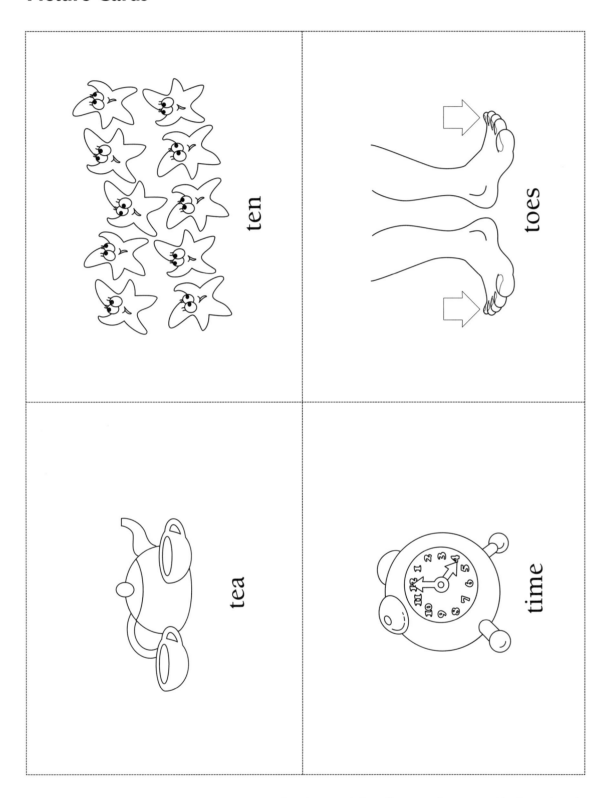

ten

toes

tea

time

Picture Cards

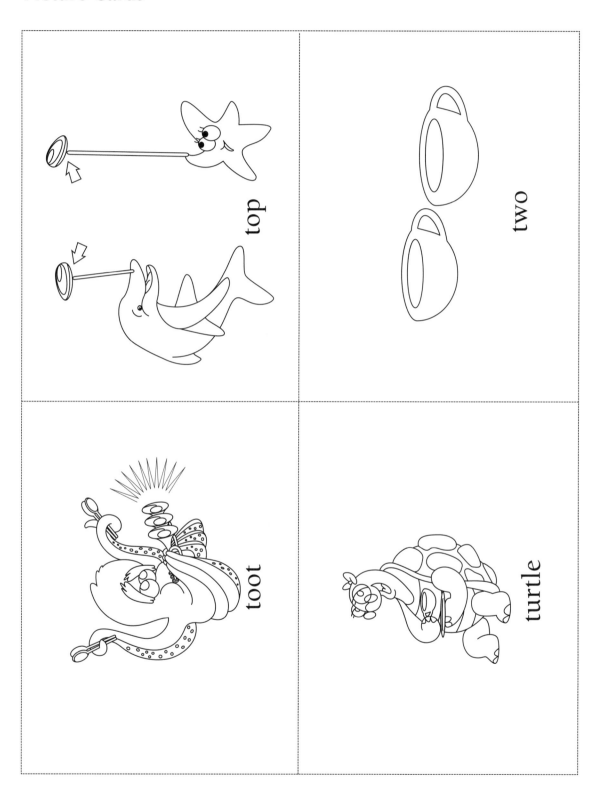

top

two

toot

turtle

Picture Cards

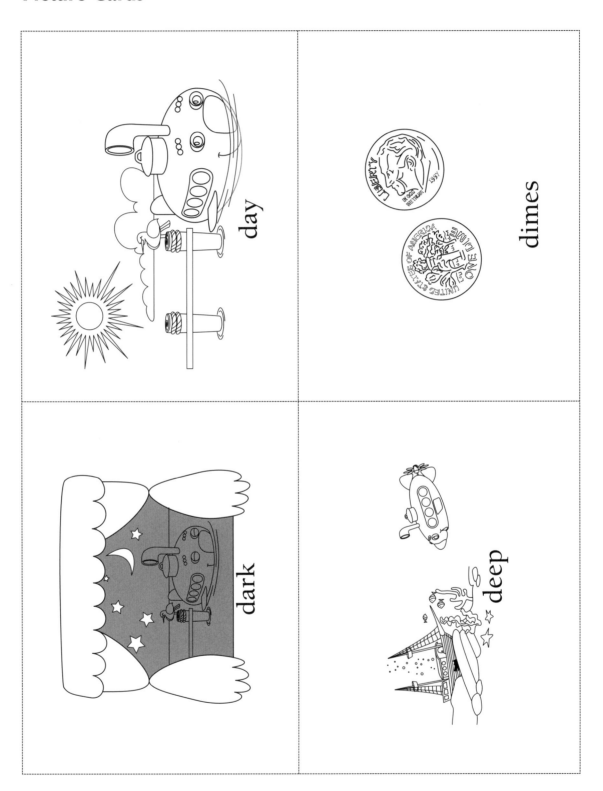

day

dimes

dark

deep

Picture Cards

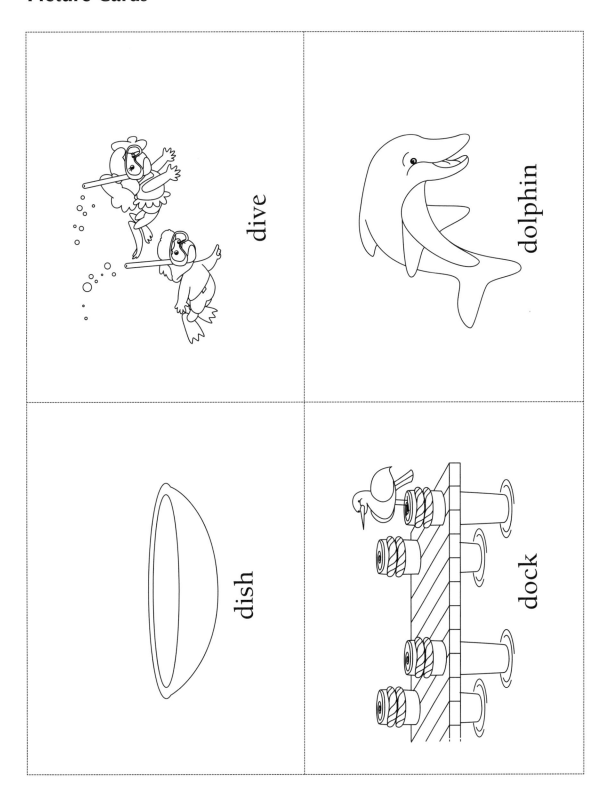

dive

dolphin

dish

dock

Picture Cards

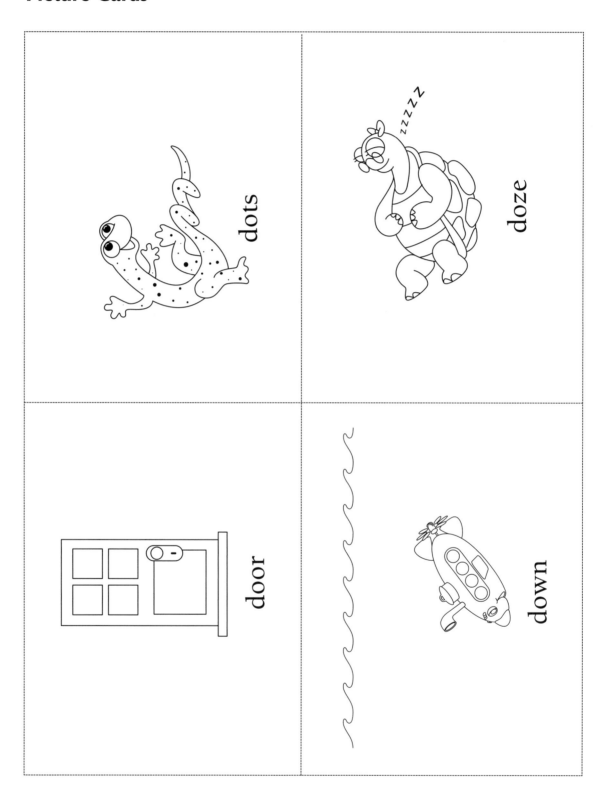

dots

doze

door

down

Picture Cards

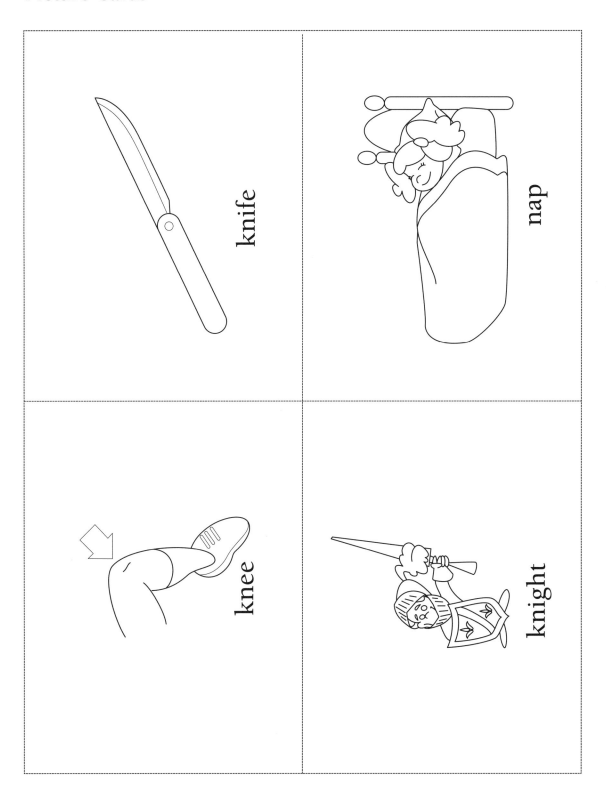

knife

nap

knee

knight

Picture Cards

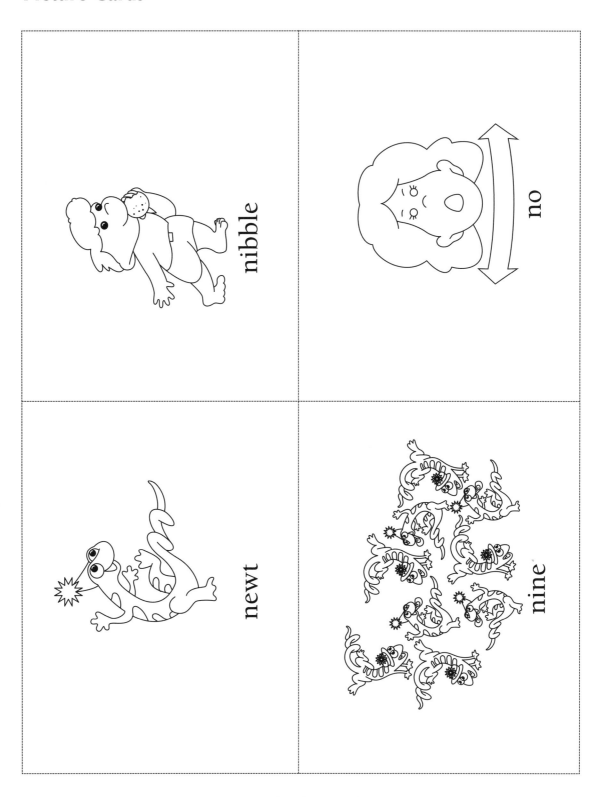

nibble

no

newt

nine

Picture Cards

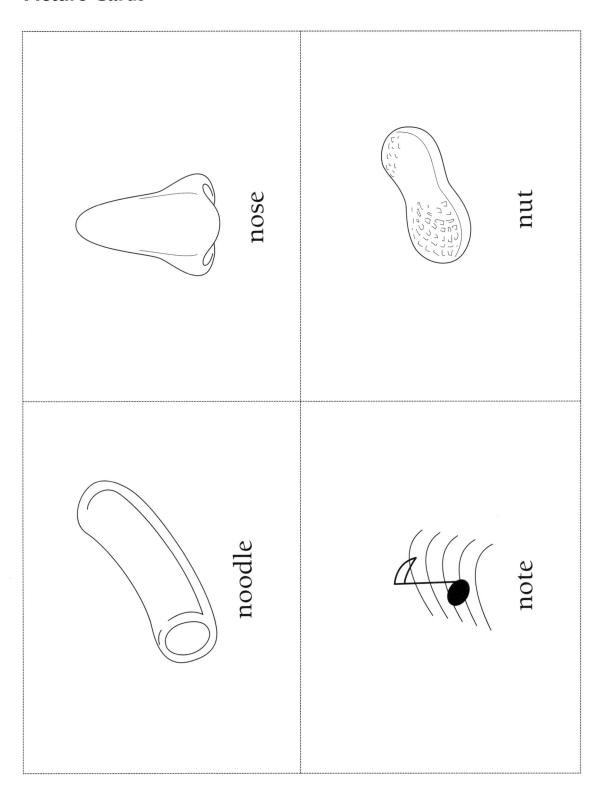

Word Count Lists

Initial /t/		Initial /d/		Initial /n/	
Word	**Frequency**	**Word**	**Frequency**	**Word**	**Frequency**
tails	1	dark	1	knock	1
takes	1	Dave	1	named	3
taking	1	dazzles	1	nap	1
tall	1	dead	1	neighbors	1
tap	1	deep	3	Nellie	1
tardy	1	dirty	1	neon	1
tea	1	diving	2	new	6
ten	1	dock	1	newts	1
terrific	1	dolphin	1	next	1
tick	6	Don	2	nibble	1
tickling	1	door	1	nice	1
time	3	down	2	nifty	1
tired	1	doze	1	nine	2
to	6	due	1	no	1
tock	6			noodle	1
toot	1			now	1
top	1				
tour	1				
tunes	1				
turtle	1				
two	2				
Total Words: 39		**Total Words: 19**		**Total Words: 24**	

Picture Card Lists

Initial /t/		Initial /d/		Initial /n/	
tail	tall	dark	day	knee	knife
tap	tape	deep	dimes	knight	nap
tea	ten	dish	dive	newt	nibble
time	toes	dock	dolphin	nine	no
toot	top	door	dots	noodle	nose
turtle	two	down	doze	note	nut

Production Practice and Carryover Activities

- Fill a **tub** with water and place items that start with /t/, /d/, and /n/ in the bottom. **Dive down deep** with your hands and tell what you find.

- Place target picture cards in an empty **tub** and have children **take** a picture out. Have them **tell** what they found, starting with a carrier phrase such as *I went diving down deep and I found….*

- Cook **noodles** for a snack and **nibble** them. Try cutting the **noodles** with a **knife**.

- Create a **die** or spinner with the **numbers two, nine**, and **ten** on it. Roll or spin to determine how many items to count out.

- Use sticker **dots** or draw **dots** to create **dot-to-dot** pictures.

- Have a **tea** party with Gertrude the **turtle**.

- Stack blocks on **top** of each other to make a **tall tower**.

- Draw sea creatures. Spin a spinner or roll a **die** to see how many **tails** to draw on them.

- Tape target picture cards on a clock. Choose a **time** on the clock and have children use the target word to **tell** what they do at each **time** of the **day** according to the clock. (Drink **tea** with a **turtle**. **Tap** with a stick. **Toot** a horn.)

- **Tap tunes** with spoons or sticks. Have children perform for each other or imitate each other's sequence of **taps**. Count and **tell** the **number** of **taps**.

Extension Activties

Rhyming

- Do these words rhyme? (yes or no)

ten - two	down - deep
tock - dock	noodle - doodle
no - toe	dark - shark
turtle - dolphin	time - clock
tap - nap	new - blue

- Which words rhyme?

tea - bee - not	toot - arm - boot
house - more - door	tap - pink - nap
tock - stick - tick	tail - belly - jelly
eight - nine - dine	sticks - tea - tricks
sub - rub - top	ship - tip - cup

- Tell a word that rhymes with *two, door, tea, night, no, deep, dish, toot, ten, dark.*

Vocabulary Development

- Read the story and discuss vocabulary that may be new to students: *submarine, starfish, reef, dolphin, newt, tour, doze, hosted, balancing, dazzles, nifty, tardy, neon, dead* (multiple meaning), *jamming out.*

Absurdities

- Present individual sequence cards and talk to students about the absurdities in the pictures. *Can an octopus really play a trumpet? Can starfish balance clams on sticks? Do turtles have tea parties?*

Classification

- Present various animals or objects. Classify items as belonging in the water or not in the water.

Present Progressive Verbs

- Use the story or sequence cards to elicit present progressive verbs by asking what the different characters are doing: *walking, diving, drinking, twirling, swimming, playing, jamming, sleeping, dreaming.*

- Act out the story and have children tell what actions they are doing in each part.

Sequencing

- Give simple directions for children to sequence the picture cards to plan a new submarine trip. For younger children, use only two or three pictures. Increase the number of pictures according to individual ability levels. Use terms such as *first, second, next,* and *last* to tell the sequence. Allow children to create their own trip sequence and explain it to you using the same terms.

Critical Thinking

- Present children with pictures of a variety of items to consider taking on a submarine trip. Have children decide which would be appropriate and explain why they chose or didn't choose the items.

- Have children compare and contrast the different water animals in the story: octopus, starfish, dolphins, clams, turtles, newts.

- Ask students what their favorite water animal is and have them explain why.

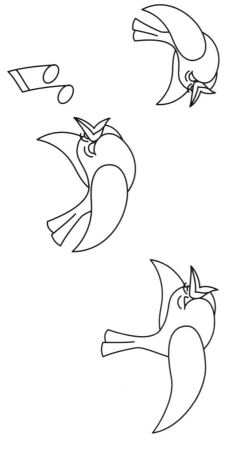

When snow starts to thaw
and birds begin singing,
when the forest awakes
and flowers start springing.

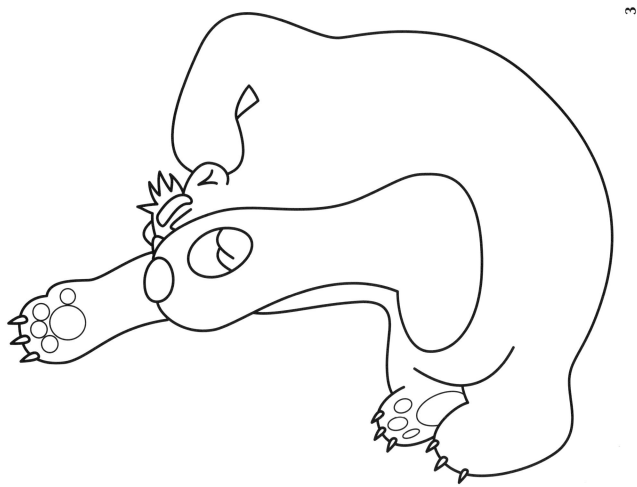

Big Bear wakes up
from his long winter snooze
with a snort and a snarl
and the hungry bear blues.

"I'm as hungry as a bear!"
he growls, his lips smacking.
"Time to head out
and do some bear snacking!"

"I may have dozed off
way back in December,
but all forest critters
had better remember…"

"I'm THE KING OF THE FOREST!"
His roar shakes the ground.
"Nothing scares me—
I'm the baddest around!"

Big Bear sets out
to smell out a victim,
but a snail on the trail
quite nearly trips him.

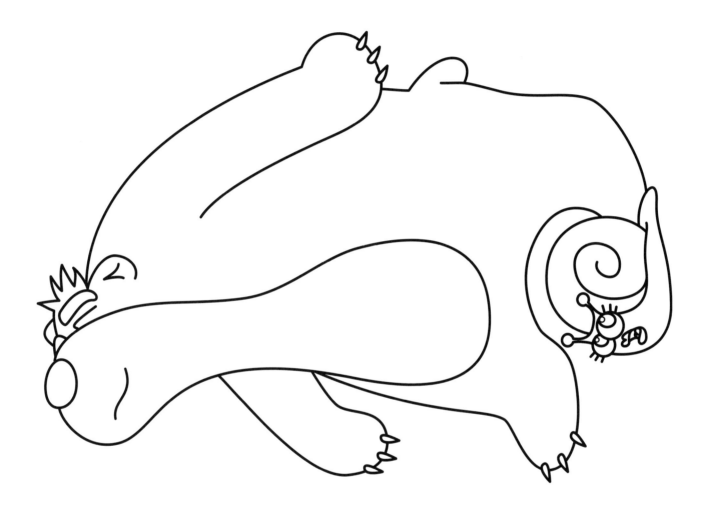

Big Bear snarls
and snorts his snortiest,
"Who dares to trip
THE KING OF THE FOREST?"

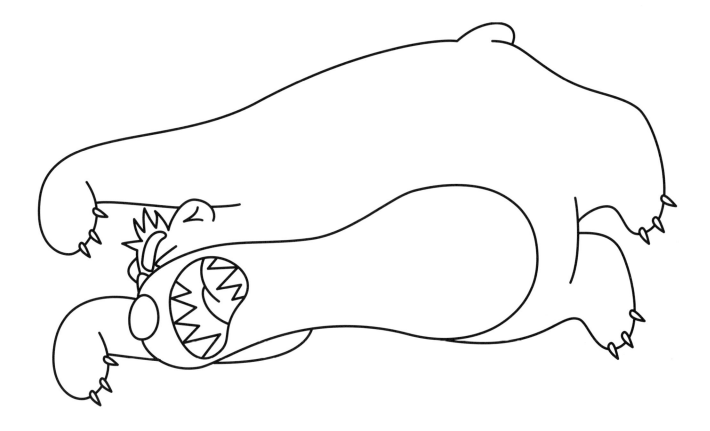

"Eeek!" squeaks the snail,
leaping out of her shell.
And Big Bear just smiles,
"That first scare went well."

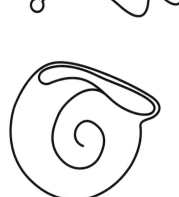

They each have a sandwich
complete with fine ham
smeared with peanut butter
and smothered with jam.

He goes back to sniffing
for something to munch
and comes upon raccoons
fixing their lunch.

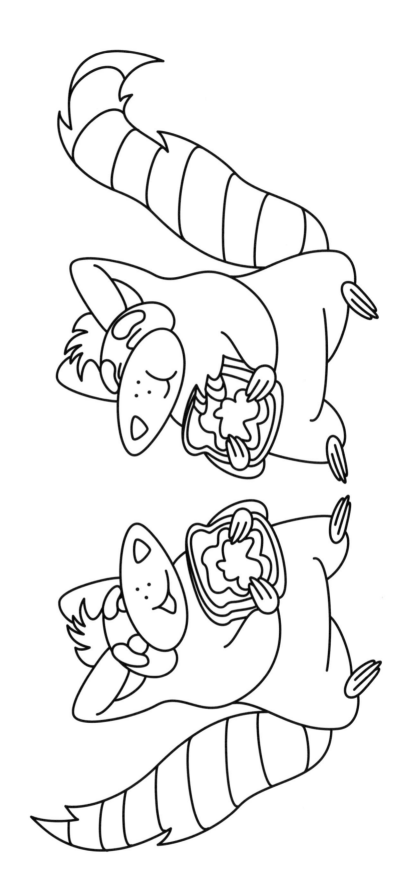

"What a snap!"
Big Bear snickers,
and smacks his bear lips.
"I'll crash from the bushes
and watch them do flips!"

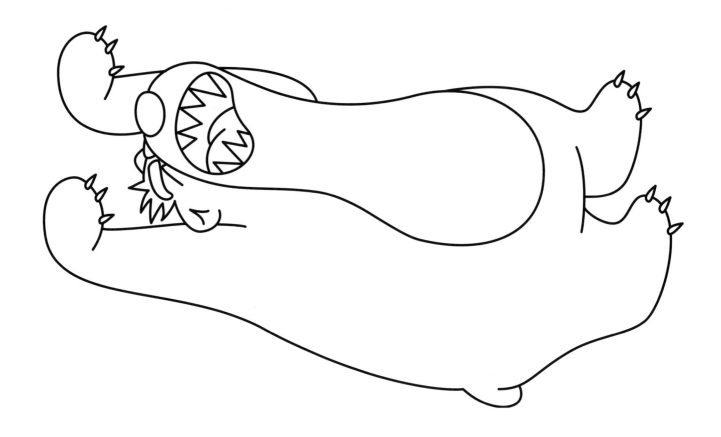

He smashes and snarls
and snorts his snortiest,
"Your lunch is now claimed
by THE KING OF THE FOREST!"

"Yipes! Holy smokes!"
are the raccoons' cries.
They abandon their food
and run for their lives.

"Ha! That was easy,"
says the bear with a sneer
and snatches the sandwiches
and slurps their root beer.

As Big Bear looks 'round
for a good spot to eat,
he spots a snake
in a very fine seat.

The snake is napping
on a stone in the sun.
But Big Bear decides
the snake snooze is done.

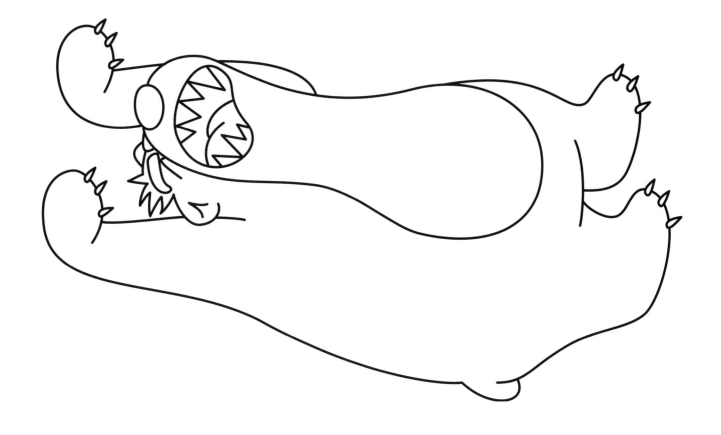

He sneaks up and snarls
and snorts his snortiest,
"Get out of the seat
of THE KING OF THE FOREST!"

The snake cries out
and snaps to upright.
"A bear! My goodness!"
then slips off in fright.

When the bear is done feasting,
he smacks his fat lap,
stretches out on the stone,
and takes a short nap.

He dreams he is walking.
on a bright sunny day,
when a bigger bear jumps out
and gets in his way.

Big Bear squeals
and cries out, "Oh my!
This bear is much bigger
and scarier than I!"

Big Bear wakes up
with a "Yikes!" and a wail.
Frightened and running,
he trips on the snail.

"Thank heavens!" he sighs,
"I was just dreaming
a much bigger bear
had sent me off screaming."

He grumbles and scowls
and snorts not-so-snortiest,
"This teaches a lesson
to the king of the forest."

"I'll respect all the creatures,
—the big and the small—
Being scared isn't fun.
It's no fun at all."

The snail, the snake, and
raccoons agreed,
"Being good friends
is what we all need."

Big Bear smiles.
He will do his bear best.
And everyone cheers
THE KING OF THE FOREST.

Sequence Cards

Sequence Cards

Sequence Cards

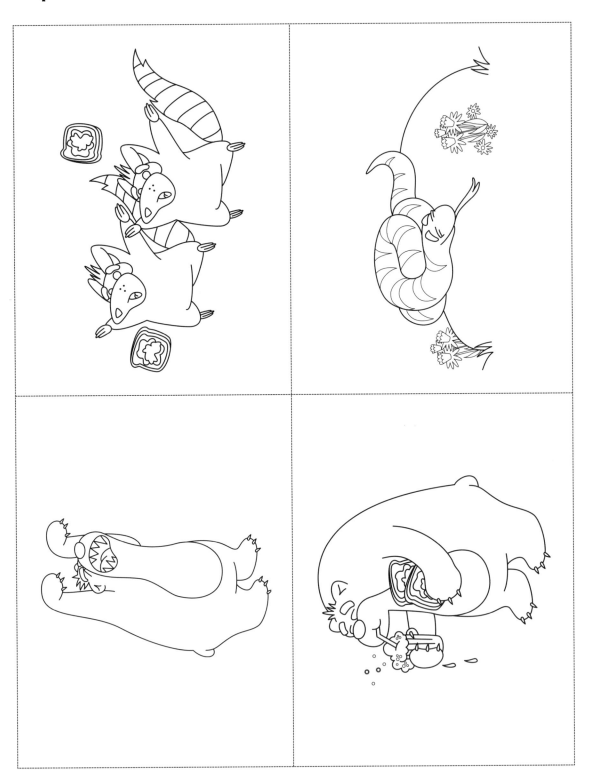

Sequence Cards

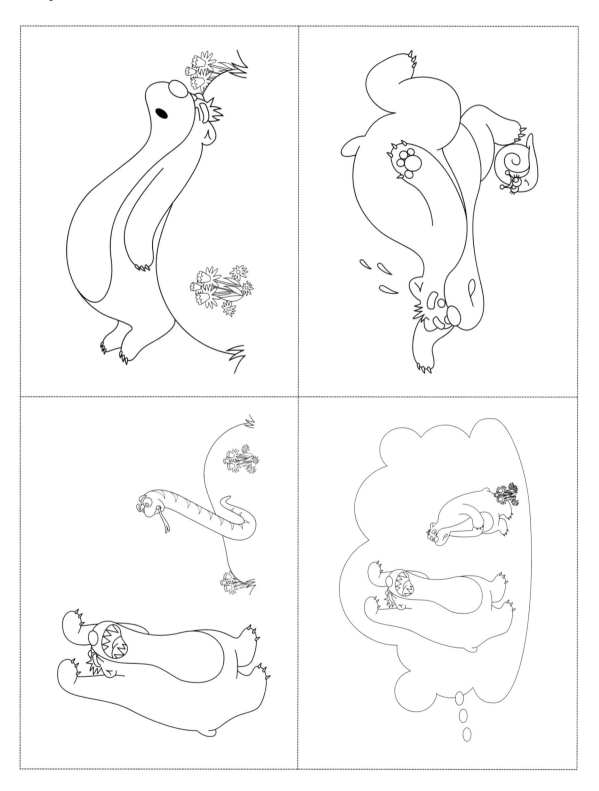

Sequence Cards

Picture Cards

small

smash

smack

smart

Picture Cards

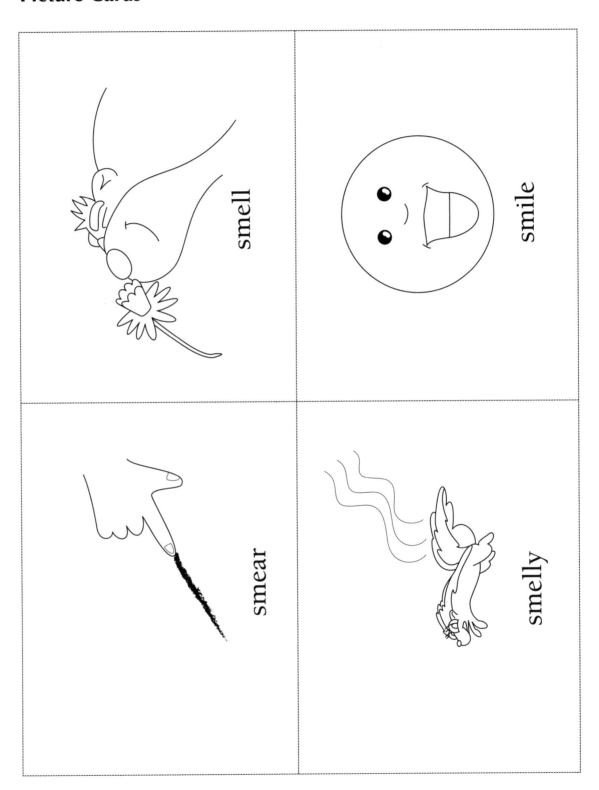

smell

smile

smear

smelly

Picture Cards

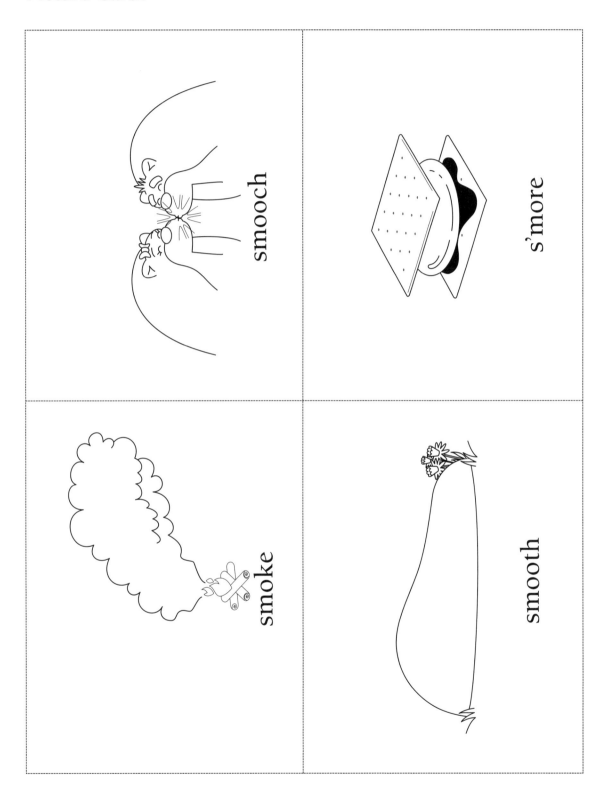

smooch

s'more

smoke

smooth

Picture Cards

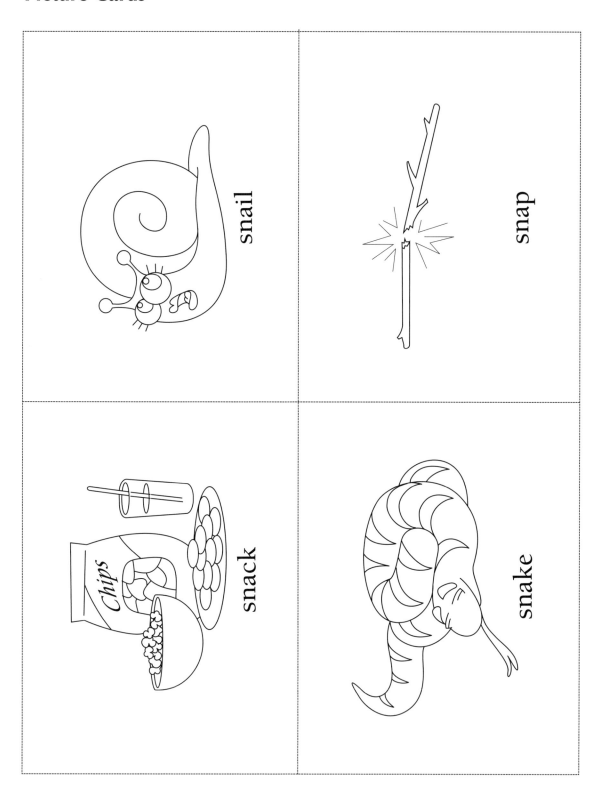

snail

snap

snack

snake

Picture Cards

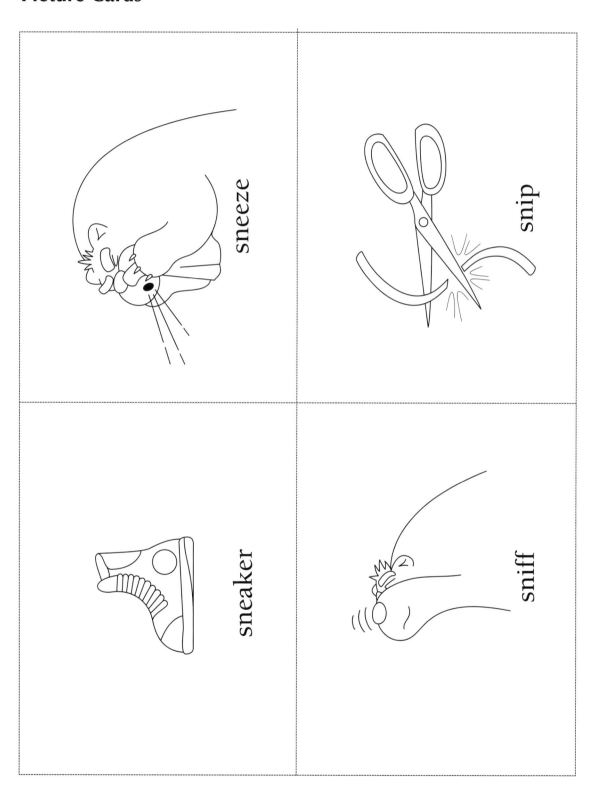

sneeze

snip

sneaker

sniff

Picture Cards

snout

snowman

snooze

snow

Word Count Lists

Initial /sm/		Initial /sn/	
Word	**Frequency**	**Word**	**Frequency**
smacking	1	snacking	1
smacks	2	snail	4
small	1	snake	5
smashes	1	snap	1
smeared	1	snaps	1
smell	1	snarl	1
smiles	2	snarls	3
smokes	1	snatches	1
smothered	1	sneaks	1
		sneer	1
		snickers	1
		sniffing	1
		snooze	2
		snort	1
		snortiest	4
		snorts	4
		snow	1
Total Words: 11		Total Words: 33	

Picture Card Lists

Initial /sm/	Initial /sn/
smack	snack
small	snail
smart	snake
smash	snap
smear	sneaker
smell	sneeze
smelly	sniff
smile	snip
smoke	snooze
smooch	snout
smooth	snow
s'more	snowman

Production Practice and Carryover Activities

- Create a path through a pretend forest using the **/sm/** and **/sn/** target picture cards. Use toy bears or plastic bear figures and have them walk through the forest. Name the various pictures along the path.

- **Sneak** to different places (e.g., the bathroom or to the door).

- Take turns **sneaking** and scaring each other.

- **Snip** paper with scissors. **Snip** a piece of green paper so that it looks like grass. Tape a string through the grass to make a **snake**.

- Make **snakes** and **snails** with modeling clay.

- **Snap** different items of clothing (e.g., coats, shirts, or pants).

- **Smear** peanut butter and jelly on bread for a **snack**.

- **Smell** different things (e.g., spices, flowers, lemons, or perfume).

- Feel **smooth** and rough objects.

- Draw a **smiley** face at the top of a piece of paper. Fill the paper with pictures of things that make you **smile**.

Extension Activities

Rhyming

- Do these words rhyme? (yes or no)

smile - snake	sneer - smear
smell - tell	smoke - rock
snail - pail	smear - smart
fort - snort	smack - snack
snap - snip	toe - snow

- Which words rhyme?

snow - chair - toe	jelly - snack - smack
snooze - scare - lose	crash - snail - trail
head - snow - bow	sneeze - finger - bees
snap - spoon - cap	small - see - tall
trip - sneak - peek	shell - snail - tell

- Tell a word that rhymes with *small, snail, snake, sneak, smell, snare, snatch, sneeze, smoke, smack.*

Vocabulary Development

- Read the story and discuss vocabulary that may be new to students: *feast, critters, victim, thaw, doze, snooze, abandon, devour, slurp, snicker, sneer, scowl, wail.*

Synonyms

- Point out common synonyms for several of the new vocabulary words: *feast-meal, critters-animals, doze-nap-sleep-snooze, devour-eat, snicker-laugh, scowl-frown, wail-cry.*

Past Tense Verbs

- Use the story pages or sequence cards to elicit both regular and irregular past tense verbs by asking what the different characters did: *growled, smacked, roared, tripped, scared, leaped, smeared, dropped, slurped, napped, tickled, hissed, cheered, sang, woke, ate, ran, drank, slept, sat.*

Critical Thinking

- Present social situations in which people are not getting along. Brainstorm solutions to solve the problems.

- Have children share personal experiences in which they were bothered by someone else. Talk about how they reacted and what the outcomes were. Discuss other actions they could have taken and what the outcomes may have been.

School

STRANGE STUFF
WE SPOT ON OUR WAY TO

Mom and I walk
the same old way
to get to my school
every day.

Speckles, my dog,
comes along for a ride.
He sits in the wagon
while I skip beside.

We stroll past stores
and vents spewing steam,
the trip uneventful
and rather routine.

Most days are quiet
and pleasant enough,
but this day we spotted
some very strange stuff.

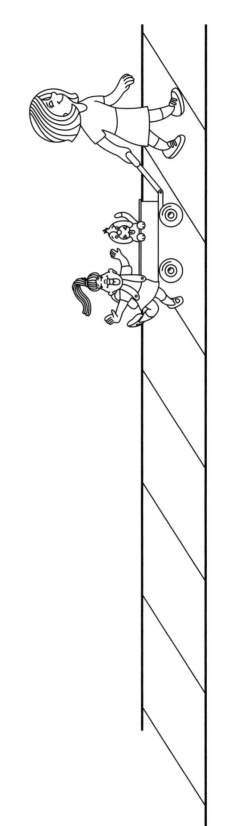

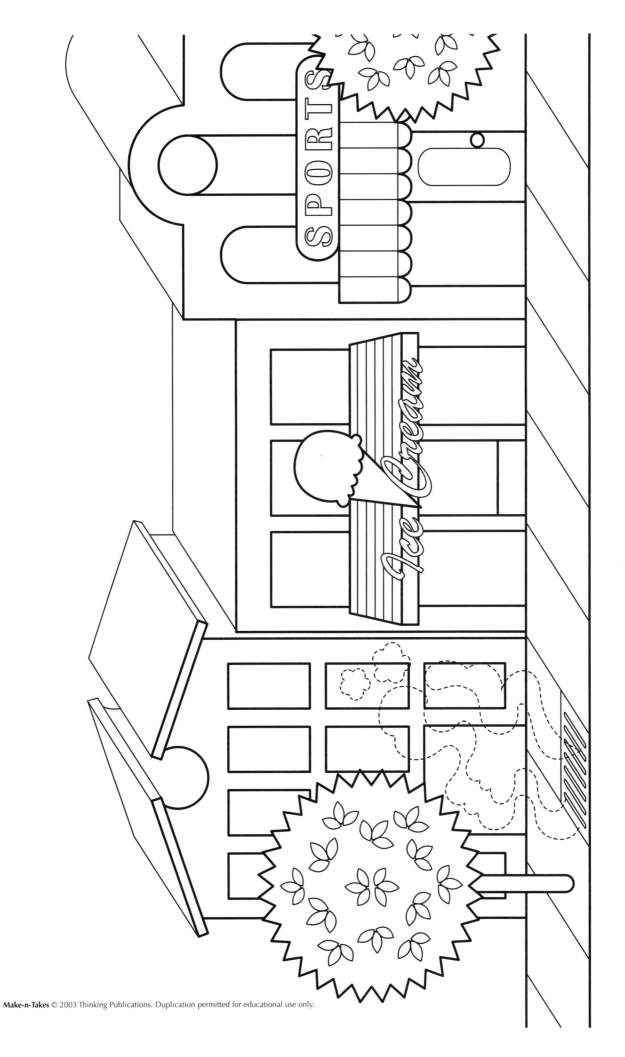

A skunk sprinted past,
right under Mom's skirt!
That event (quite unpleasant)
put us all on alert.

We stood there in shock
taking stock of our senses
when a stork flew from the sky—
barely clearing the fences.

These two events
by themselves would seem weird,
but soon even more
strange stuff appeared.

I spotted a spoon
and a scoop filled with ice cream.
Mom spied a sponge
and step stool for cleaning.

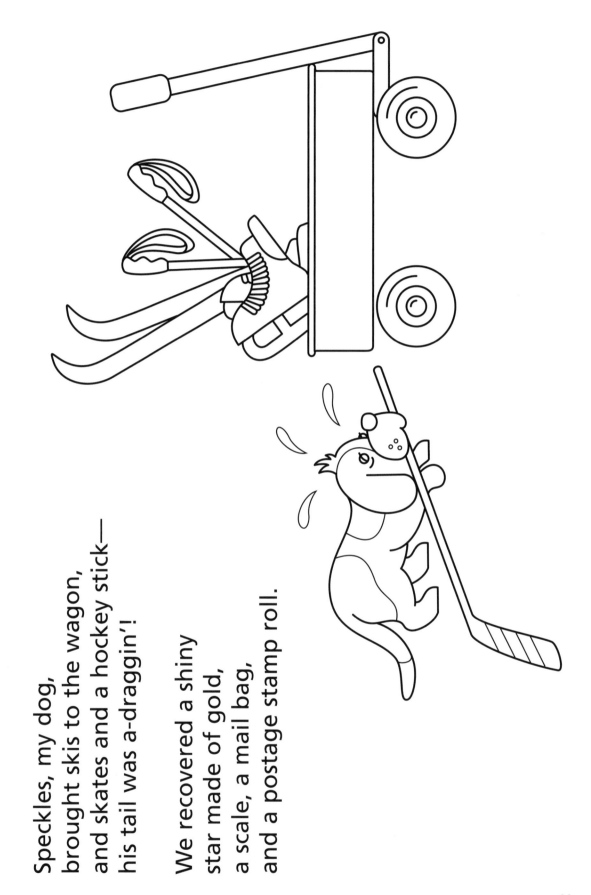

Speckles, my dog,
brought skis to the wagon,
and skates and a hockey stick—
his tail was a-draggin'!

We recovered a shiny
star made of gold,
a scale, a mail bag,
and a postage stamp roll.

Strange stuff we spotted
made quite a stack.
Mom pulled in front
while I pushed in back.

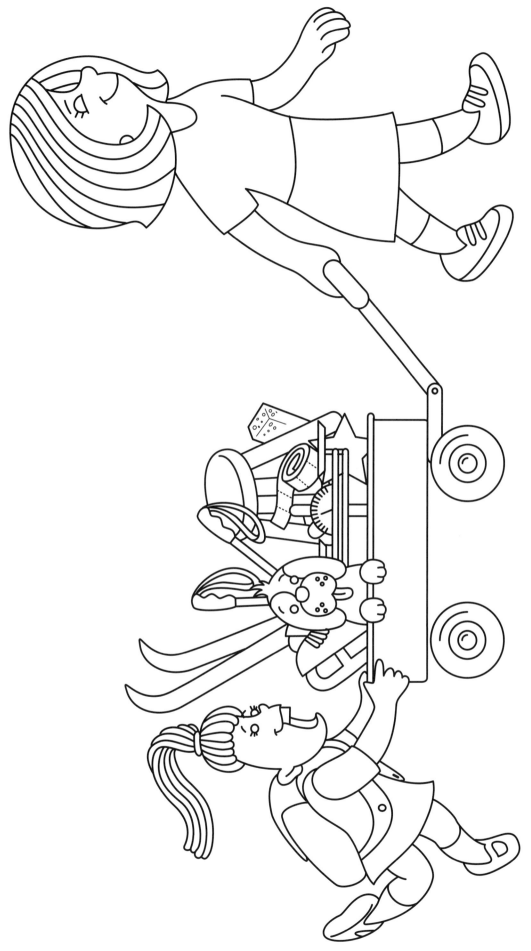

We made it to school
and discovered a swarm
of angry folks shouting,
creating a storm.

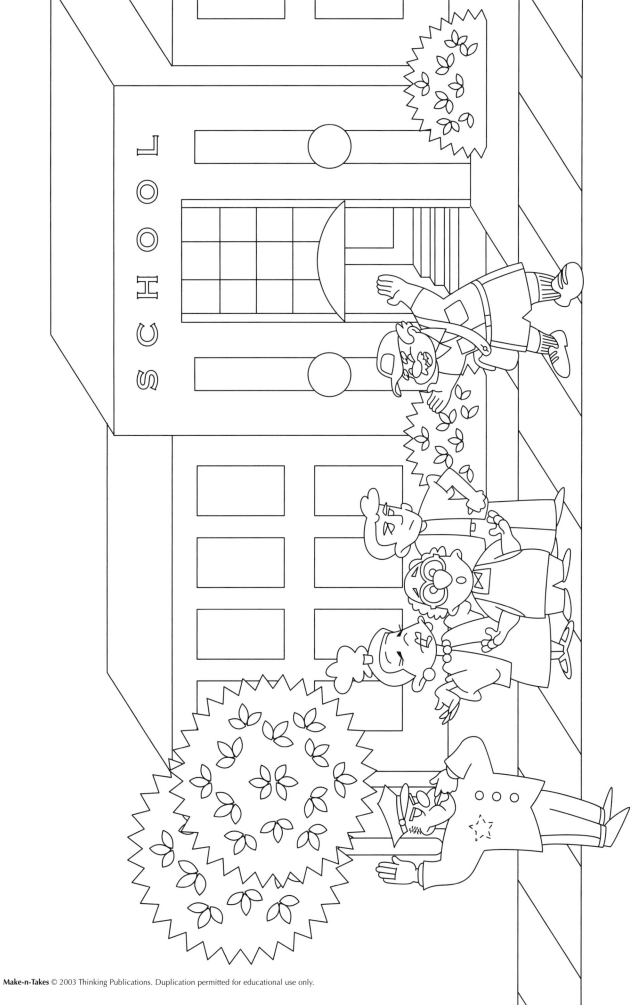

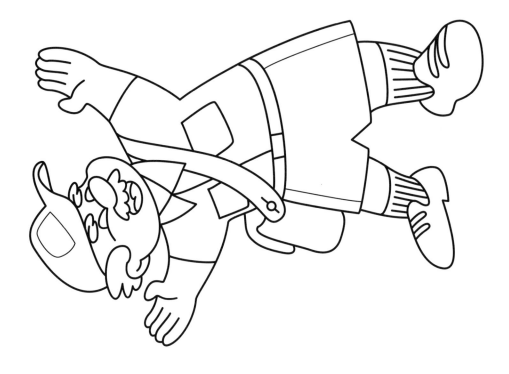

A mailman declared,
"I'll deliver no mail
if I can't recover
my stamps and my scale."

Three shopkeepers shouted
above all the fuss,
"We'll go out of business.
What about us?"

A cop tried vainly
to get them to listen.
His efforts were useless—
his gold star was missing!

Amidst the confusion
and noise all around,
a zookeeper's truck
parked by the school ground.

"Has anyone seen
a stork and a skunk?
They slipped out the door
with a 'whoosh!' and a 'clunk!'"

"They ran through the streets
and maybe a shop.
They knocked down a mailman
and a cop yelling 'STOP!'"

I suddenly realized
the strange stuff we had
was part of the reason
these folks were so mad.

The cop and the mailman got all their stuff back that scattered about in the stork/skunk attack.

The shopkeepers smiled and nodded when told that all of their items could once more be sold.

The step stool and sponge would once more help clean the window displaying scoops of ice cream.

The skates and hockey stick, one owner reports, are back on display for those who play sports.

26

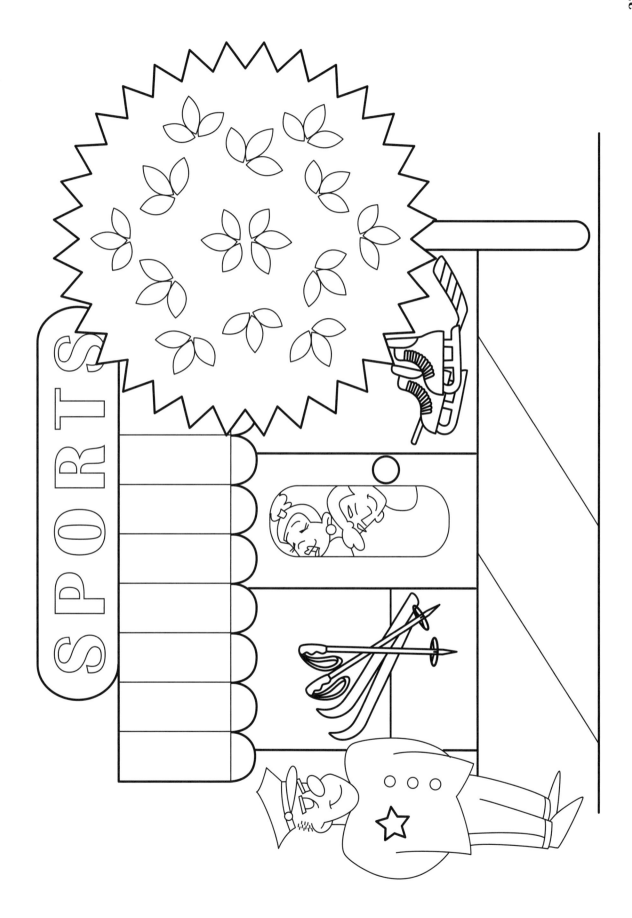

SPORTS

SPORTS

What of the zookeeper?
Well—she's happy, too.
The stork and the skunk
returned to the zoo!

Sequence Cards

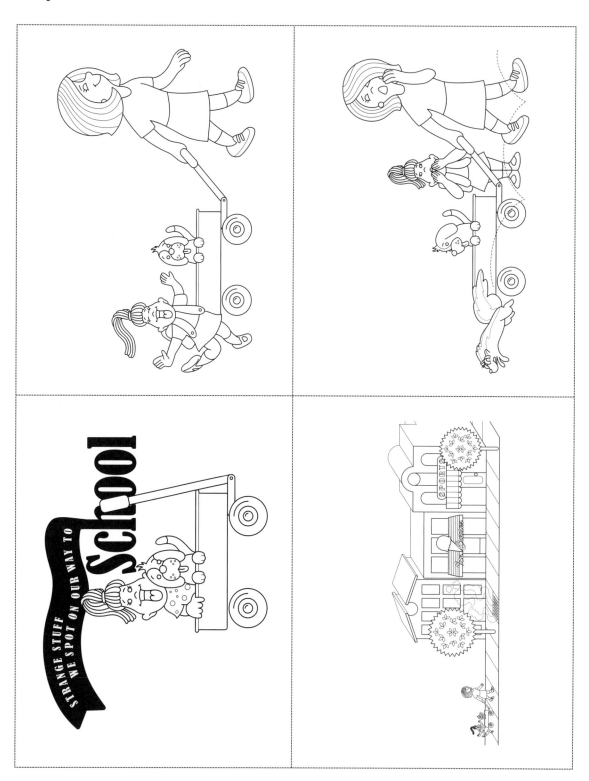

Sequence Cards

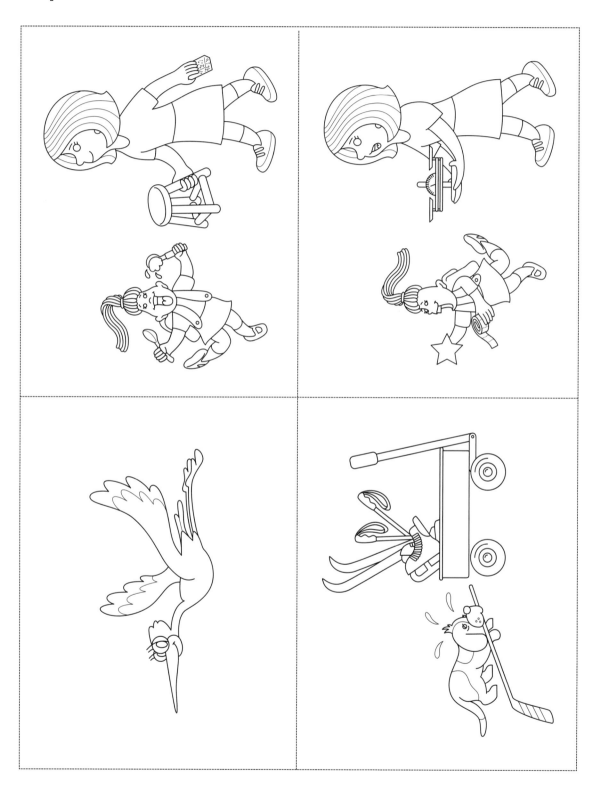

Sequence Cards

Sequence Cards

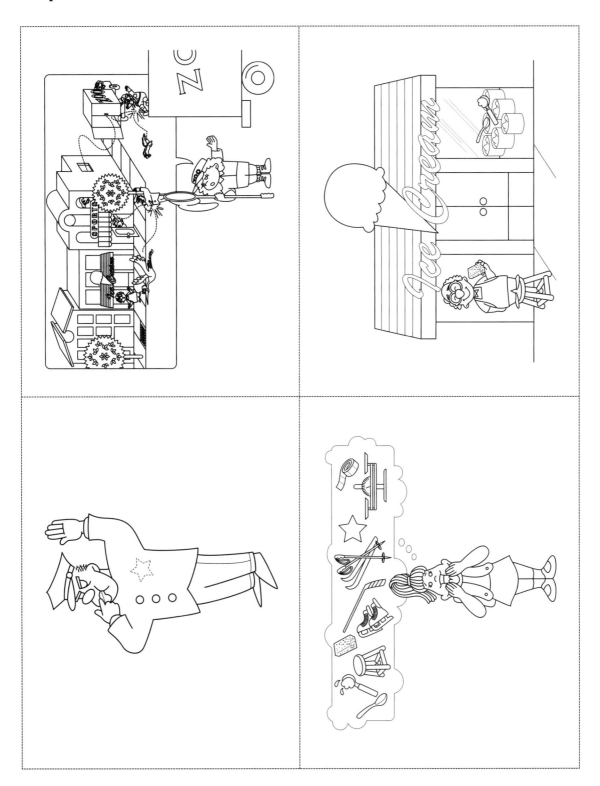

Make-n-Takes

Sequence Cards

Picture Cards

spear

spill

sparkle

spider

Picture Cards

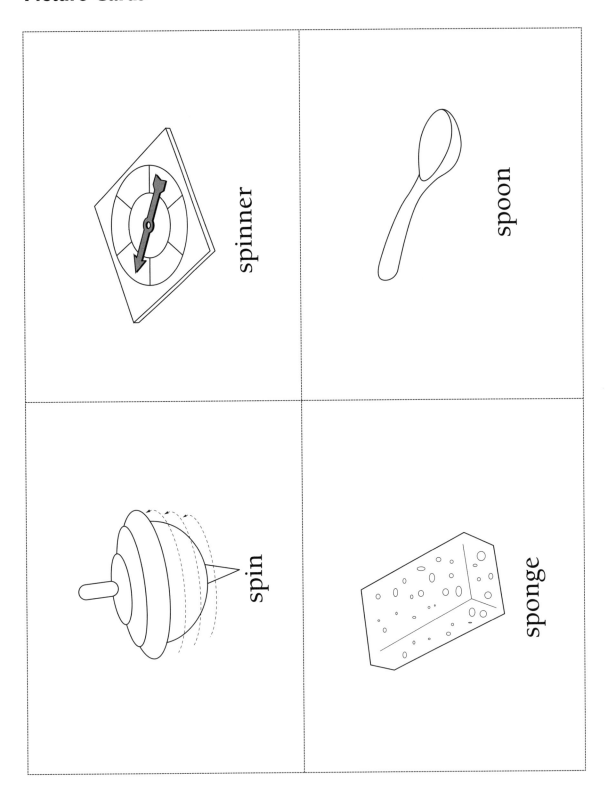

spinner

spoon

spin

sponge

Picture Cards

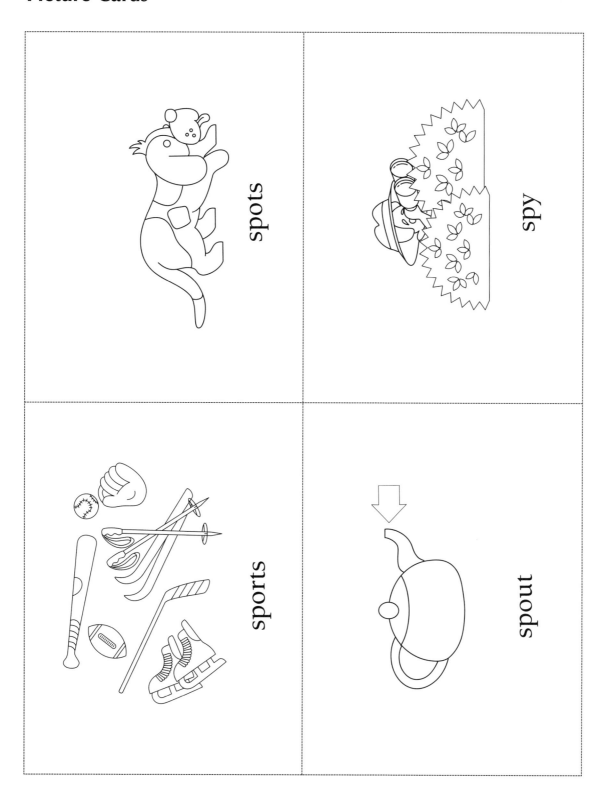

spots

spy

sports

spout

Picture Cards

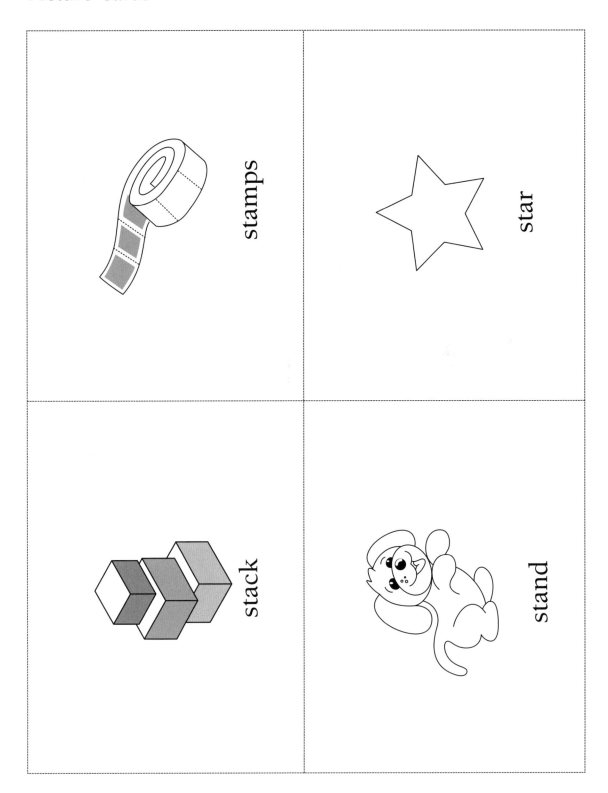

stamps

star

stack

stand

Picture Cards

step

stool

steam

stick

Picture Cards

store

storm

stop

stork

Picture Cards

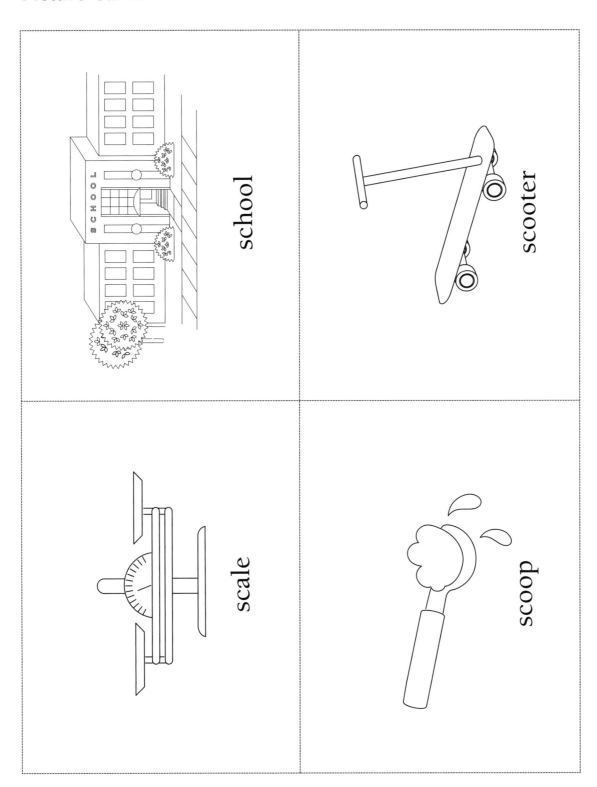

school

scooter

scale

scoop

Picture Cards

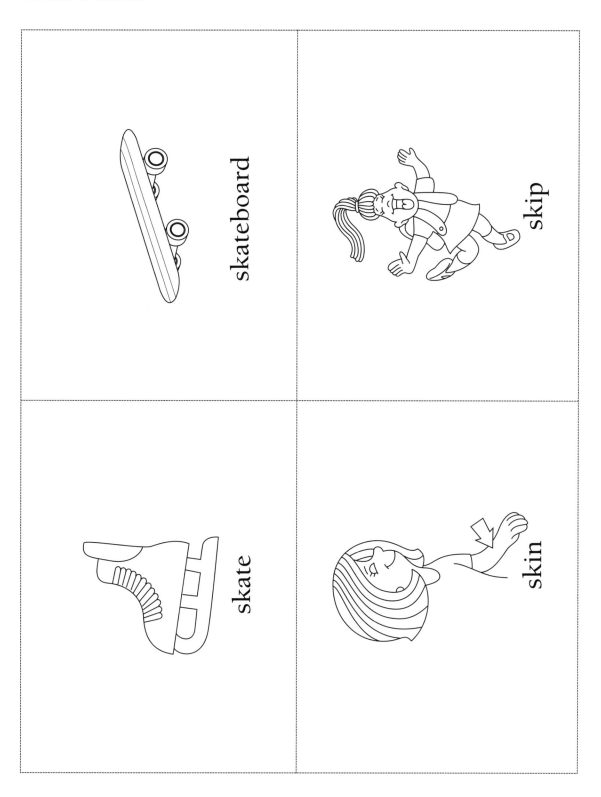

skateboard

skip

skate

skin

Picture Cards

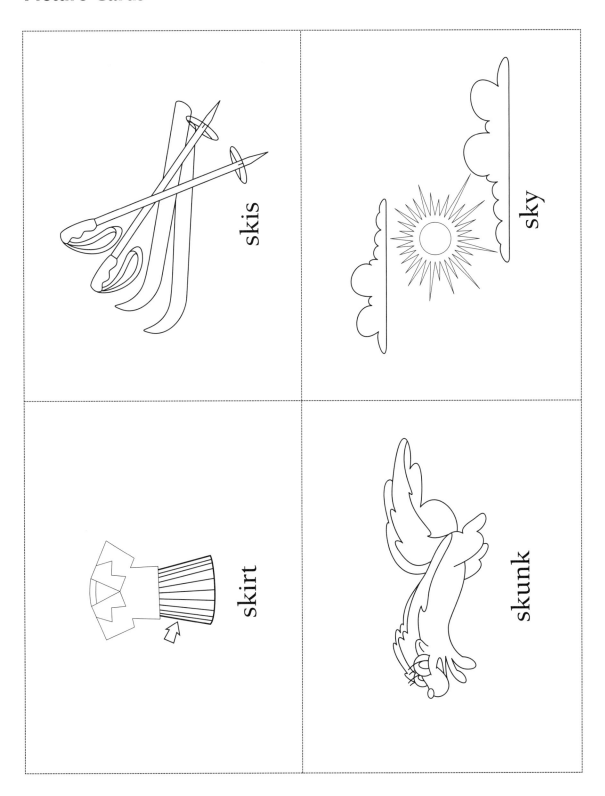

skis

sky

skirt

skunk

Word Count Lists

Initial /sp/		Initial /st/		Initial /sk/	
Word	Frequency	Word	Frequency	Word	Frequency
speckles	2	stack	1	scale	2
spewing	1	stamp	1	scattered	1
spied	1	stamps	1	school	3
sponge	2	star	2	scoop	1
spoon	1	steam	1	scoops	1
sports	1	step	2	skates	2
spotted	3	stick	2	skip	1
		stock	1	skirt	1
		stood	1	skis	1
		stool	2	skunk	4
		stop	1	sky	1
		stores	1		
		stork	4		
		storm	1		
		stuff	5		
Total Words: 11		Total Words: 26		Total Words: 18	

Picture Card Lists

Initial /sp/	Initial /st/	Initial /sk/
sparkle	stack	scale
spear	stamps	school
spider	stand	scoop
spill	star	scooter
spin	steam	skate
spinner	step	skateboard
sponge	stick	skin
spoon	stool	skip
sports	stop	skirt
spots	store	skis
spout	stork	skunk
spy	storm	sky

Production Practice and Carryover Activities

- Hide target pictures or objects beginning with **/sp/**, **/st/**, and **/sk/**. Take a walk and **spot** the items. Collect them in a wagon. Name the items found.

- Draw a dog on a chalkboard. Take turns **spinning** a **spinner** to determine the number of **spots** or **speckles** to add to the dog. Name the dog **Spot** or **Speckles**.

- Take a walk and use binoculars to **spot** objects. **Spot** things on the ground and in the **sky**.

- Make milkshakes or sundaes using an ice cream **scoop**. Count the **scoops** of ice cream. Eat with **spoons**.

- **Sponge**-paint a picture. Use shapes to make a picture of the **sky**.

- Create a large circle using target picture cards. **Skip** around the circle. Sing *Skip to My Lou*. When the song is over, name the picture closest to you.

- Write letters and **stamp** envelopes with ink **stamps**. Use real **stamps** and mail the letters.

- **Skate** or ride **scooters** to retrieve target pictures or objects.

- Count **steps** on a **stairway**. Place picture cards on the **steps** and say the names of the pictures as you go up or down the **steps**.

- Use a balance **scale** to compare weights of target objects.

Extension Activities

Rhyming

- Do these words rhyme? (yes or no)

spill - will	star - car
spin - skip	stool - mule
spoon - moon	skin - tin
spot - ski	scoop - hoop
stamp - steam	skunk - smell

- Which words rhyme?

stool - spin - fin	stack - pack - step
spider - stop - cop	skip - spill - hip
sports - spear - hear	skirt - dirt - steam
spot - hot - stick	skunk - sky - trunk
scale - pail - weigh	skate - date - sponge

- Tell a word that rhymes with *spill, spoon, spot, steam, store, stick, star, school, skip, sky.*

Vocabulary Development

- Read the story and discuss vocabulary that may be new to students: *alert, display, scale, steam, swarm, routine, spewing, stroll, sprinted, recover, vainly, scattered, taking stock.*

Associations

- Present pictures or real objects from the story and discuss who would use them.

- Play a guessing game. Have children guess who you are according to the objects you tell them you use.

Functions

- Present pictures or real objects from the story. Discuss the uses of the various objects found in the story.

- Put pictures or objects in a container. Take turns choosing an object or picture and telling its function so that someone else can guess what was chosen.

Possessives

- Use the storybook illustrations or sequence cards to talk about items and who their owners are. Elicit various possessive forms with models and direct questions. For example, *Whose stamps are these?* (the mailman's stamps, his stamps) or *Speckles belongs to the little girl. Whose dog is Speckles?* (hers, the girl's dog).

Critical Thinking

- As you read the story, have children guess who may have lost the various objects that are found.

- Have children look at the various people in the illustrations and hypothesize about why each person is upset or what each person may be missing. Discuss why the items are important to the characters and what might happen when those items are lost.

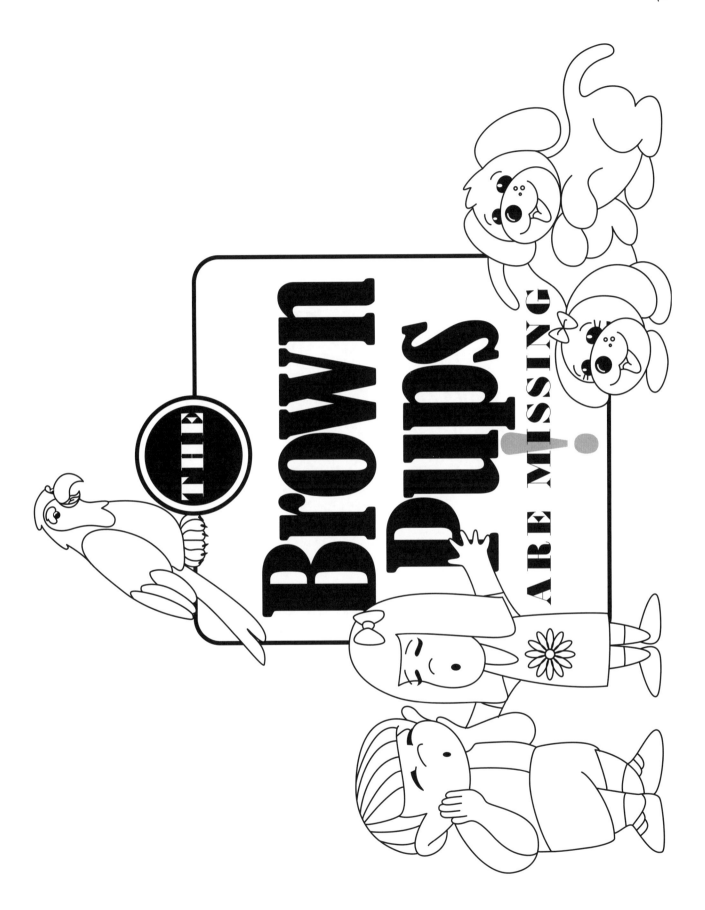

THE Brown Pups ARE MISSING

We went to the pet shop
on the far edge of town
to pick up two beautiful
new pups of brown.

But the pups we had come
to buy here today
are no longer in
the pet shop's display.

Over our weeps,
our wails, and our whines,
a parrot named Pops
pipes in with these lines...

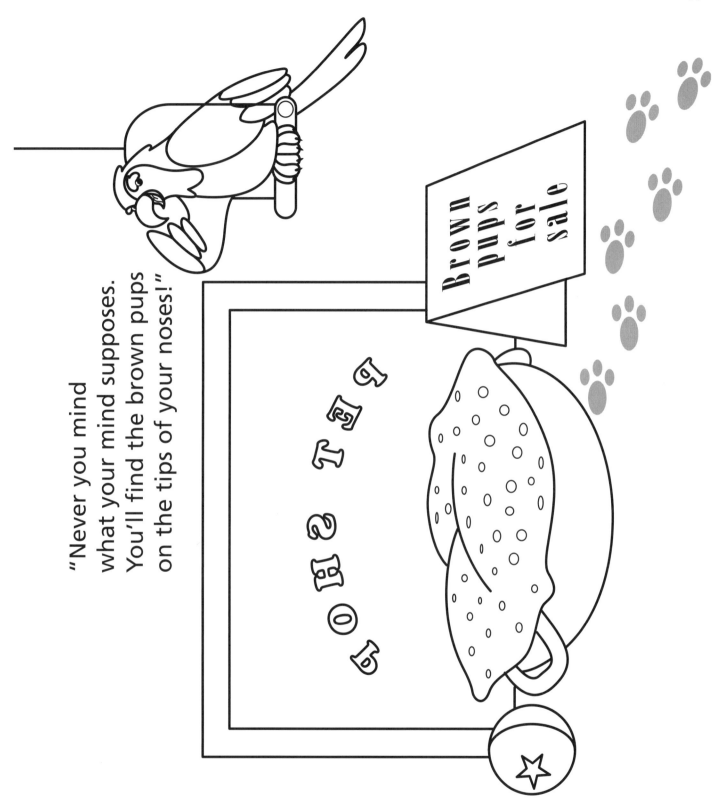

"Never you mind
what your mind supposes.
You'll find the brown pups
on the tips of your noses!"

PET SHOP

Brown pups for sale

Pops hops down,
and squawks from my shoulder,
"The search for the pups
is far from over.
Never you mind
what your mind supposes.
To find the brown pups,
just follow your noses!"

Pops raises our hopes
with this puzzling clue.
So we search for the pups.
(Pops helps out, too.)

We discover a mess
cleaned up with some mops
by waiters who work
at one of the shops.

Heaps of fine plates,
broken cups, and a tray
are scattered all over—
complete disarray.

We're sure we both know
who spilled all these cups—
the work of escaping,
excited brown pups!

4

Says Pops, "So it seems
that this is a clue,
a mess that only
escaped pups could do.
But never you mind
what your mind supposes.
The brown pups are at
the tips of your noses!"

waiters with mops
and spilt coffee trays
shout out in front
of their shops' displays.
It's clear to us
who jammed the town—
it just has to be
the small pups of brown!

Out in the street
are three angry cops
trying to fix
broken traffic stops.
Trucks and buses,
cars and bikes
are honking horns
at traffic lights

while...

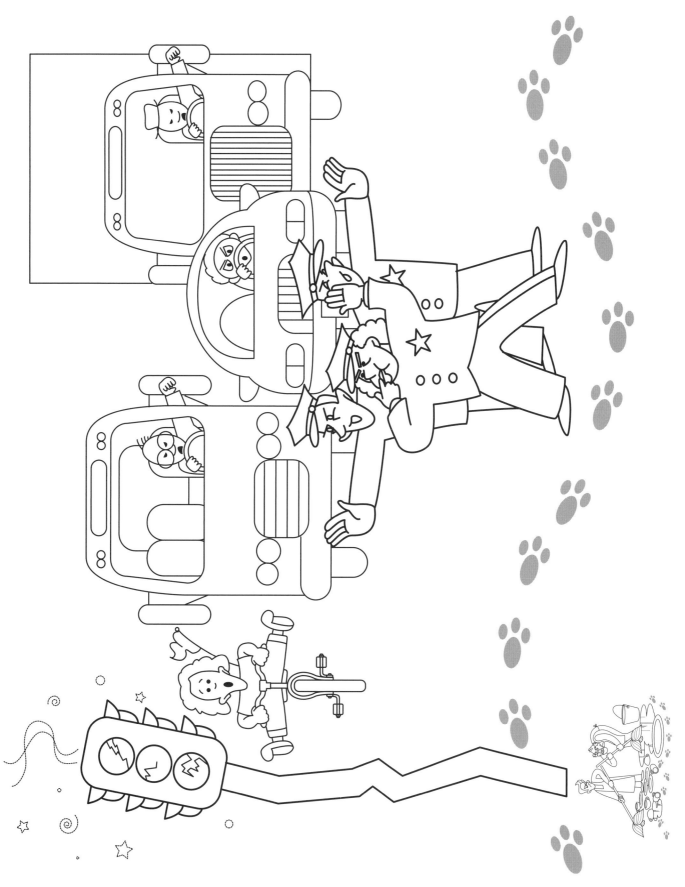

Pops chirps in
while nibbling on grapes,
"Follow the clues on
those torn drapes!
Never you mind
what your mind supposes.
You'll find the brown pups
by following your noses!"

A fruitcart tipped over
its apples and grapes,
and the dress shop
somehow
has torn its drapes

while...

a yellow bus beeps
and bugs the two cops
to hurry and fix
the broken traffic stops.
The waiters still shout
and gather up cups—
but still there's no sign
of our little brown pups.

The chaos keeps coming.
The ruckus increases.
Right near the pet shop
another mess greets us.

9

And then...

fresh bakery smell
circles around.
We'll grab a quick snack,
then cover more ground.
We open the door
to follow our noses,
to wherever the smell
of sweet pastry pulls us.

We head on inside,
smacking our lips,
thinking of cakes
and chocolaty chips.

Once we're away
from rips in the drapes,
the tipped-over cart
of apples and grapes,
away from the beeps
and cops in a hurry
to fix broken stops
that caused such a flurry,
away from the waiters
so busy with mops,
picking up cups
in front of their shops,
away from the pet store
where pups took their naps,
we realize our noses
are puppy road maps.

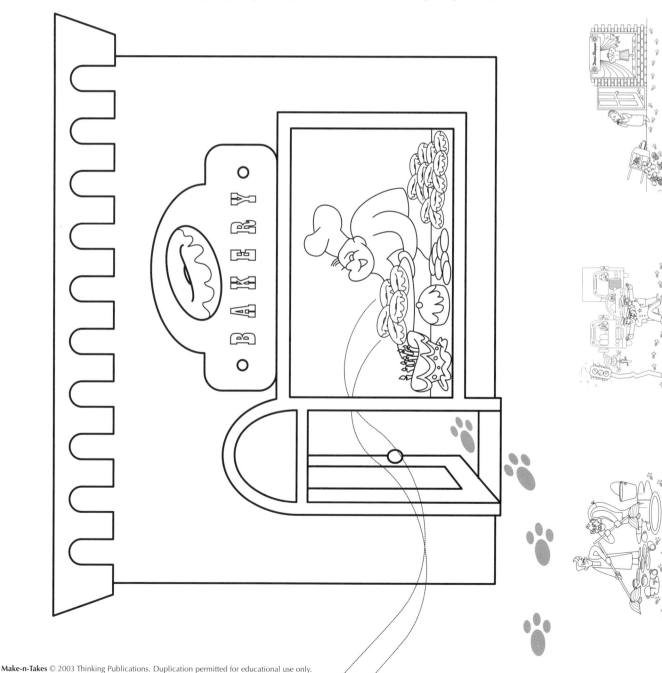

There were no more tips
nor one more clue
that could have achieved
what Pops wanted to.

Just like Pops said,
just like he told us,
we found the brown pups
by following our noses!

Sequence Cards

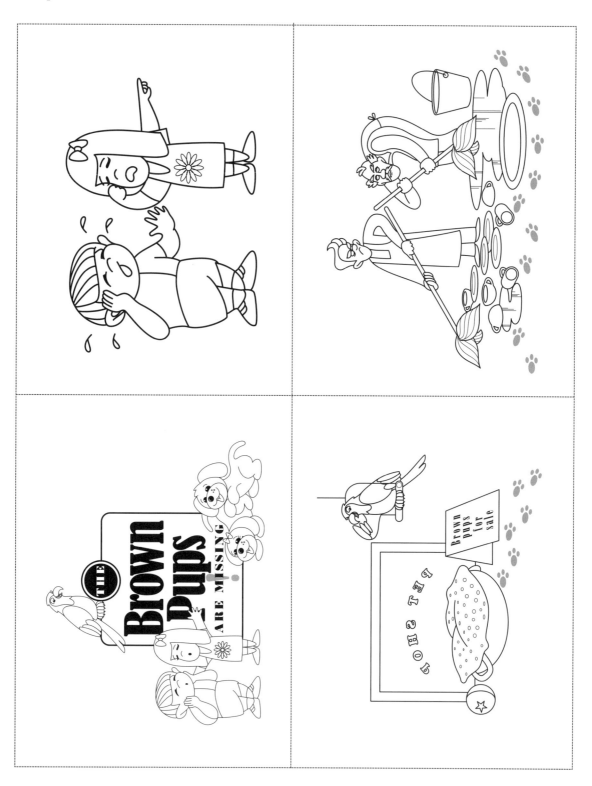

Sequence Cards

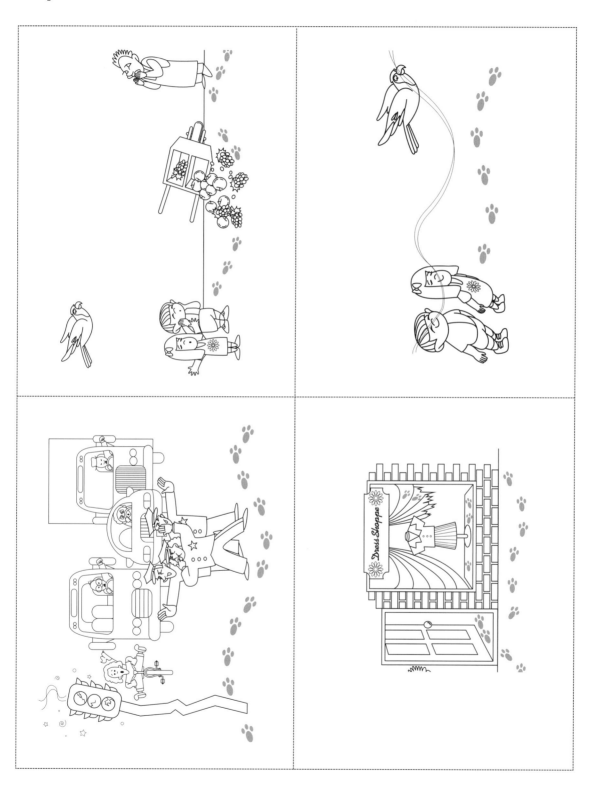

Sequence Cards

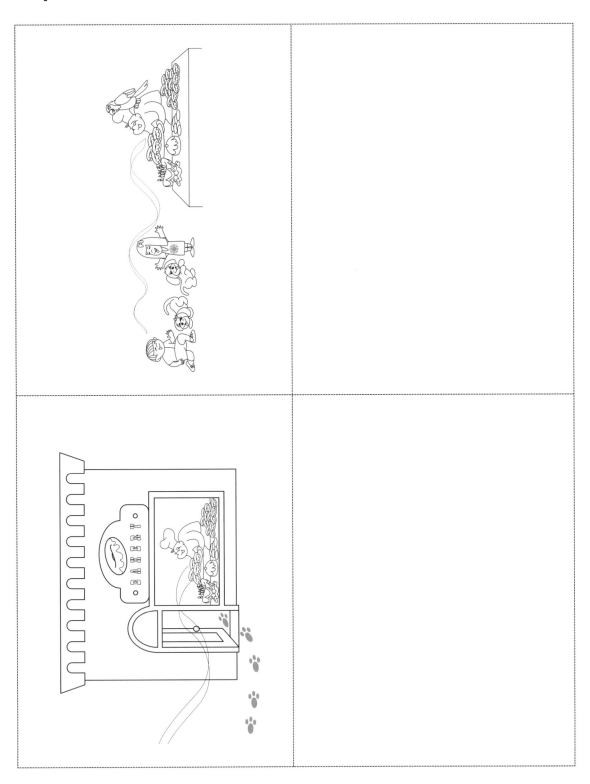

Picture Cards

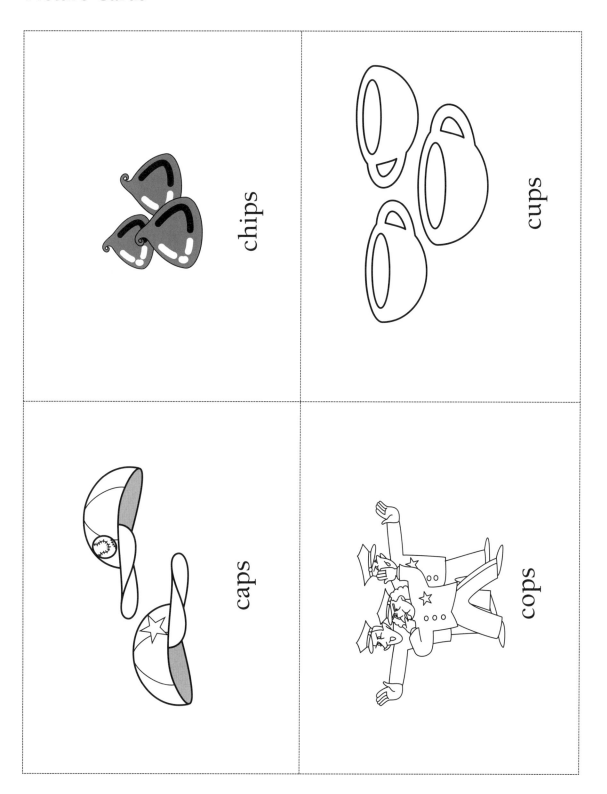

chips

cups

caps

cops

Picture Cards

lips

mops

hops

maps

Picture Cards

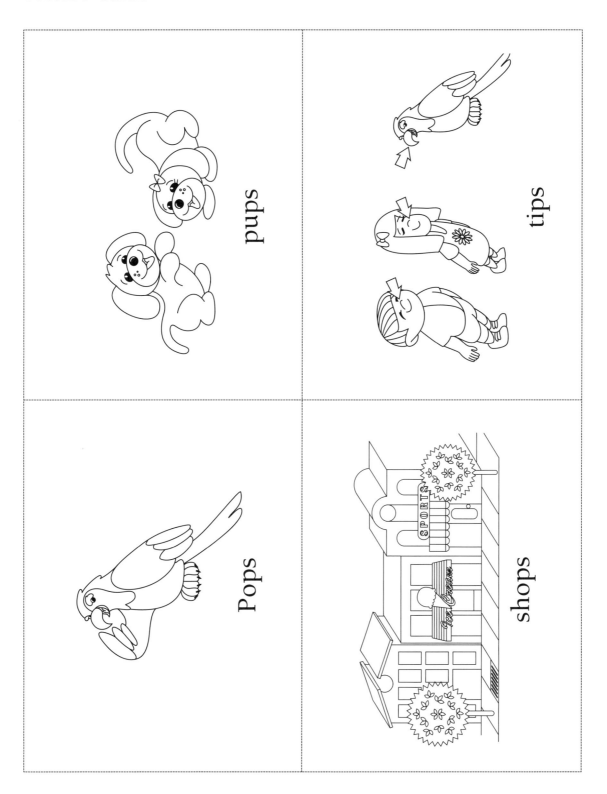

pups

tips

Pops

shops

Word Count List

Final /ps/	
Word	Frequency
beeps	2
chips	1
cops	3
cups	4
drapes	3
grapes	3
heaps	1
hopes	1
hops	1
keeps	1
lips	1
maps	1
mops	3
naps	1
pipes	1
Pops	8
pups	14
rips	1
shop's	1
shops'	1
shops	2
stops	3
tips	3
weeps	1
Total Words: 61	

Picture Card List

Final /ps/
caps
chips
cops
cups
hops
lips
maps
mops
Pops
pups
shops
tips

Production Practice and Carryover Activities

- Eat **grapes** for a snack. Have each child count out a certain number and then tell how many **grapes** he or she has.

- Stack **cups**. Count the number of **cups** you are able to stack before the stack **tips** over.

- Pretend you are looking for the lost **pups**. Have children use the picture cards to create **maps** that lead to the **pups**. Follow the **maps** to find the **pups** by taking turns stepping on each card and saying the name of the picture. Spin a spinner to determine the number of **steps** (cards) to move for each turn.

- Create a city by spreading the sequence cards depicting places from the story around the room. Spin a spinner to determine how many **steps** or **hops** should be between each picture card. Take a trip through the city. Take turns spinning to see how many **steps** or **hops** you can take to get to the next location.

- Play Captain, May I to get to the pups, and have the captain tell how many **steps** each person can take.

- Count **steps** on a stairway. Place picture cards on the **steps** and say name of the pictures as you go up or down the **steps**.

- Take turns honking horns. Spin a spinner or roll a die to determine how many **beeps** to make. Have children count the number of **beeps** they hear someone else make.

- Present the **tops** of various containers. Count the number of **tops**. Group the **tops** according to **shapes**, sizes, and colors. Have children match **tops** to their appropriate containers.

- Blow bubbles using bubble **pipes**.

- Use **mops** to wash the floor.

Extension Activities

Rhyming

- Do these words rhyme? (yes or no)

  pups - caps   weeps - beeps
  pops - cops   grapes - apples
  chips - lips   mops - stops
  rips - pipes   hopes - hops
  cups - keeps   naps - maps

- Which words rhyme?

  pups - noses - cups   bird - Pops - cops
  hops - tops - tips   pipes - beeps - cheeps
  rush - pipes - wipes   loops - hoops - town
  spill - mops - shops   rips - car - chips
  hopes - grapes - drapes nose - naps - maps

- Tell a word that rhymes with *pups, beeps, apes, tips, mops, naps, mopes, wipes, soups, shops.*

Vocabulary Development

- Read the story and discuss vocabulary that may be new to students: *bakery, pastry, drapes, clue, weeps, sobs, display, disarray, chaos, flurry, jammed, supposes, greets, escaping.*

Synonyms

- Point out common synonyms for several of the new vocabulary words: *weeps-sobs-cries, greets-meets, drapes-curtains, chaos-disarray-mess.*

Multiple-Meaning Words

- Discuss words in the story that have multiple meanings: *bugs, chips, line, pipes, pops, stops, tips.*

Plurals

- Use the sequence cards or picture cards to elicit plural forms.

Sequencing

- Refer children to the small sequence icons at the bottom of story pages to review the places the pups have been. Ask questions to reinforce children's understanding and use of sequential concepts. *Where did the pups go first? Where did they go after they tipped over the apples and grapes? What was the last place the pups went?*

Critical Thinking

- Brainstorm other places the pups could go and what might happen if they went to those places.

It's raining outside.
We're gloomy and blue.
We all whine to Mom,
"There's nothing to do!"

But Mom is unfazed—
thinks nothing of it.
She simply announces,
"Let's clean the big closet!"

Mom must be nuts!
What could she be thinking?
We trudge up the steps,
our hopes for fun sinking.

We whine, "It doesn't
seem very fair, does it?
What joy could there be
in a big, old dumb closet?"

"Let's see what's inside,"
Mom answers back.
"We'll find piles of things
to put fun back on track."

"Imagination comes
in unlimited sizes.
What's in this big closet
just might surprise us."

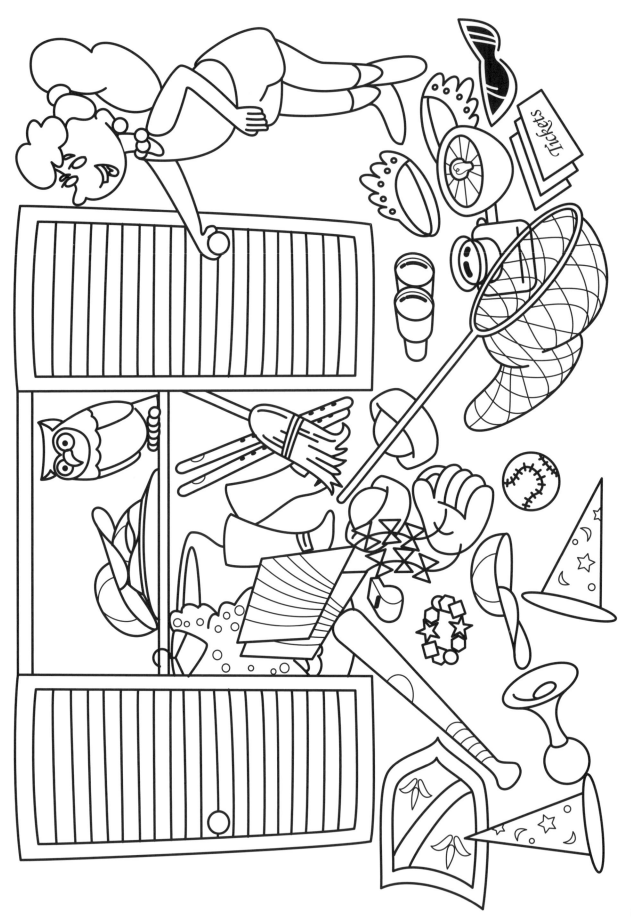

She twists the knob open
on the big closet door,
and piles of junk
crash to the floor.

The most wondrous of sights
that we've ever seen—
the biggest pile that
there's ever been!

"Hey look! Sailor hats!"
my sister Sal hoots.
"Fish nets and foghorns
and a whistle that toots!"

We make like sea captains
with fleets of big boats,
blasting our foghorns
at all that floats.

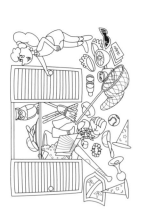

Baseballs and mitts
and fine wooden bats.
Look! Underneath!
Two baseball hats!

See the big hero!
He struts to home plate
as though he's become
a Hall of Fame great.

The bat cracks mighty
o'er the crowd's thunderous roar.
The hero comes through
for the game-winning score.

We dig out a camera,
sunglasses and boots,
coats with pink dots,
and bracelets and suits.

A fashion show! Of course—
with models and glitz.
The flashbulbs all popping
create quite a blitz.

Then we discover
some shiny pink tights,
two silver crowns,
and a shield worn by knights.

"Tie sheets in knots
and drop the rope down!
I'll leap 'cross the moat
to restore the true crown!"

The princess and queen
Sir Knight shall save.
They reward him with cookies
because he's so brave.

Binoculars and helmets!
This stuff isn't boring—
perfect accessories
for jungle exploring.

Traveling upriver
in long, skinny boats,
we see crocodiles
and strange, hairy goats.

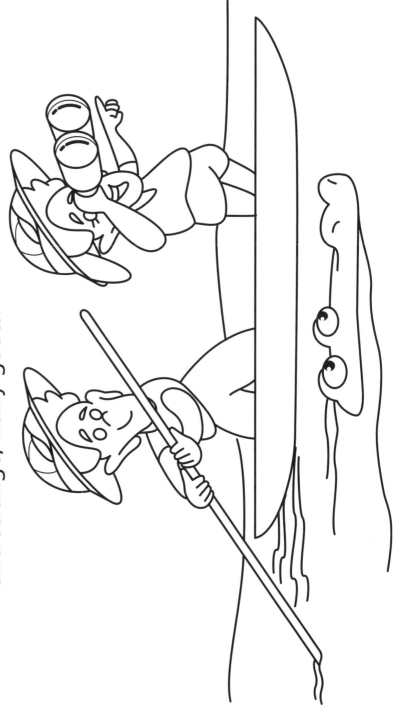

We see a small tribe
in odd-looking huts
with monkeys for pets
and sweet-tasting nuts.

A stuffed owl, a broomstick,
and large rusty pots
are ideal ingredients
for wizardly plots.

Our spell contains hog's hair
and four yellow newts.
We start the pot boiling
by playing gold flutes.

The spell is disrupted
by a bright yellow glow.
The sun has come out!
Rain's over, let's go!

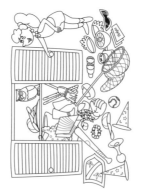

The big closet holds
its last of delights.
We scramble outside
with two rainbow kites.

We're glad to be able
to run out the door,
but we still recall
what Mom said before...

"Imagination comes
in unlimited sizes."
And the big closet proved
it held big surprises!

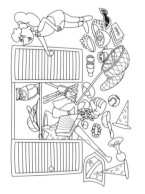

Sequence Cards

Sequence Cards

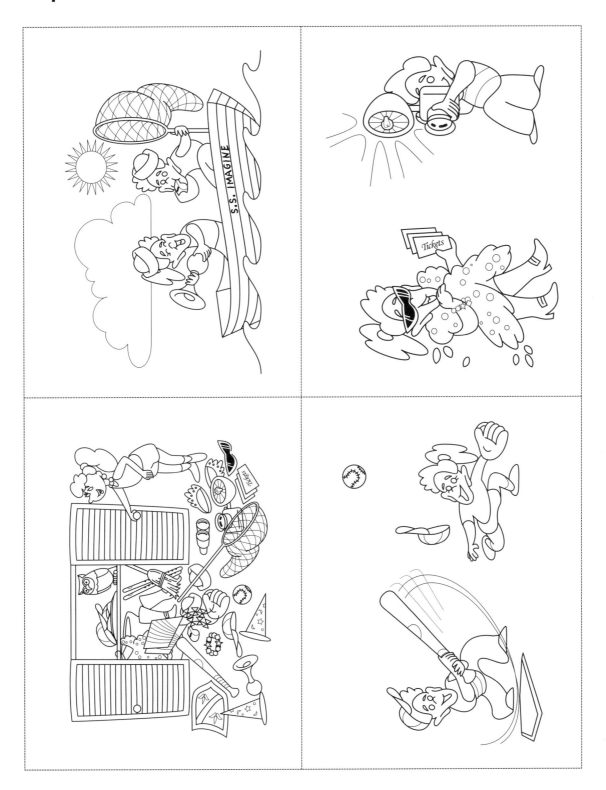

Sequence Cards

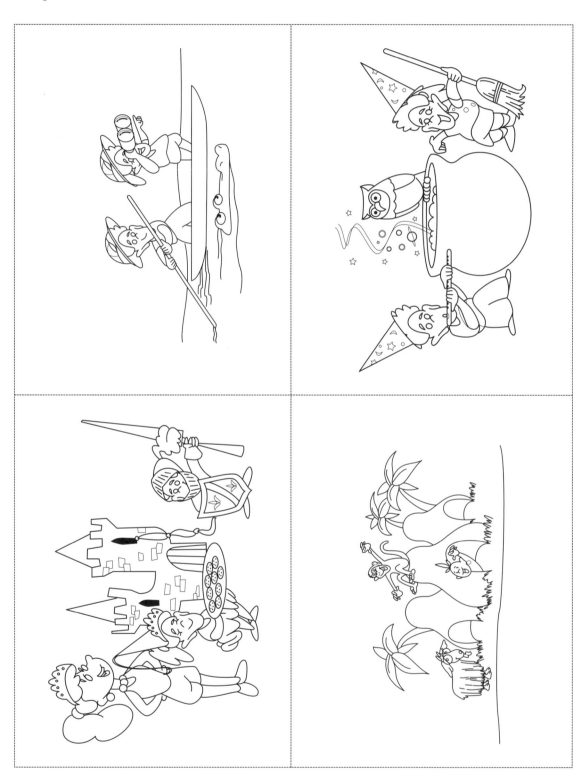

Sequence Cards

Picture Cards

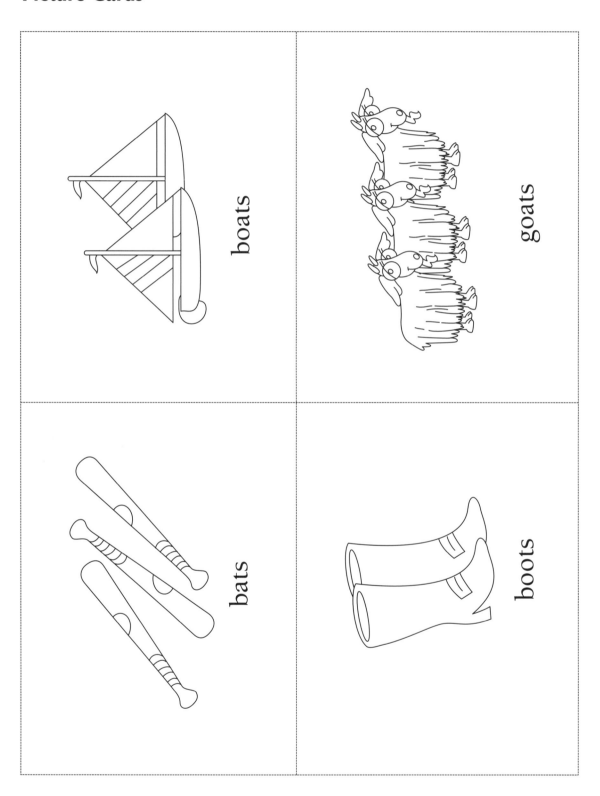

boats

goats

bats

boots

Picture Cards

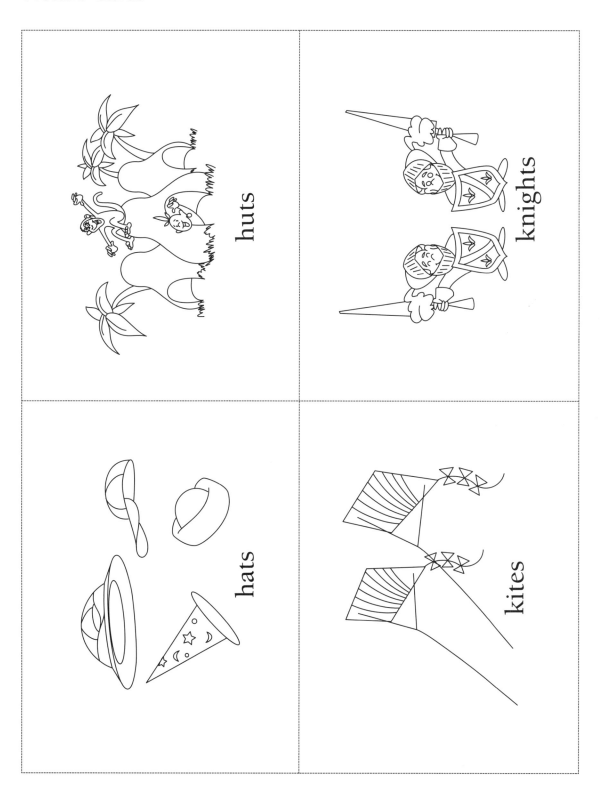

huts

knights

hats

kites

Picture Cards

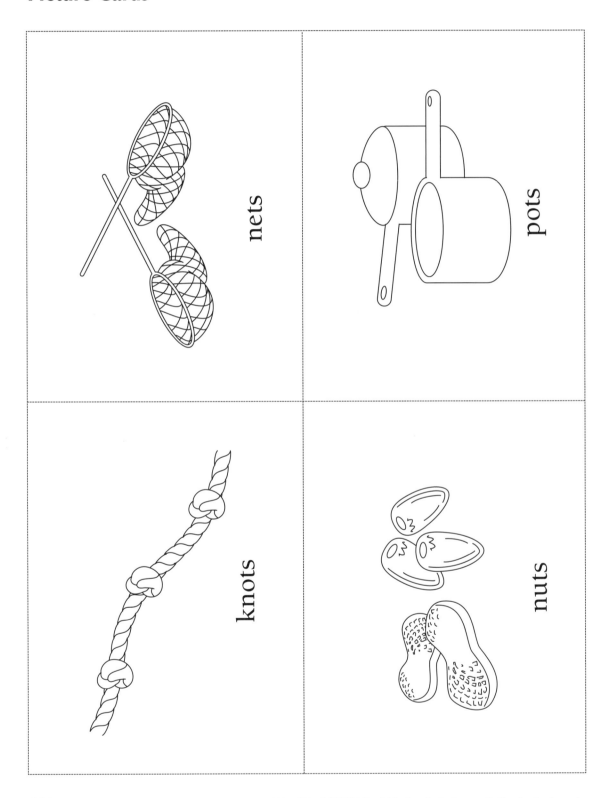

nets

pots

knots

nuts

Word Count List

Final /ts/	
Word	**Frequency**
bats	1
blitz	1
boats	2
boots	1
bracelets	1
coats	1
delights	1
dots	1
fleets	1
floats	1
flutes	1
glitz	1
goats	1
hats	2
helmets	1
hoots	1
huts	1
it's	1
kites	1
knights	1
knots	1
let's	3
mitts	1
nets	1
newts	1
nuts	2
pets	1
plots	1
pots	1
sheets	1
sights	1
struts	1
suits	1
tights	1
toots	1
what's	2

Total Words: 42

Picture Card List

Final /ts/
bats
boats
boots
goats
hats
huts
kites
knights
knots
nets
nuts
pots

Production Practice and Carryover Activities

- Use manila folders as **closets**. Place the **/ts/** target picture cards inside. Take turns looking in the **closets** and finding the pictures. Tell what things are in each closet.

- Place pairs of small objects ending with **/ts/** in a tub of water. Use small fish **nets** to catch the objects. When all the items are caught, talk about what was caught. *We caught two nuts. We caught toy **hats**. We caught a pair of **boots**.*

- Present a variety of different kinds of **nuts**. Count the number of **nuts**. Group the **nuts** according to shapes and sizes.

- Eat **nuts (peanuts)** for a snack. Have each child count out a certain number and then tell how many **nuts** he or she has. (Be aware of allergy concerns.)

- Fill a container with water. Place small objects in the water and see which things float. Have children tell what **floats** and what sinks.

- Play with toy **boats**.

- Make **kites**. Fly **kites** outside.

- Use baseball **mitts** to play catch.

- Present a variety of **hats**. Count the **hats**. Talk about who would wear the **hats**. Try wearing several **hats** at once.

- Fill a box or bag with objects that end in **/ts/**. Take turns choosing an object, naming it, and thinking of something fun to do with the item.

Extension Activities

Rhyming

- Do these words rhyme? (yes or no)

bats - tickets	boots - scoots
glitz - blitz	huts - nuts
pets - pits	flutes - floats
dots - pots	fleets - boats
knights - kites	mitts - sights

- Which words rhyme?

mitts - kits - kites	helmets - greats - waits
hoots - boats - coats	nights - nets - pets
plots - newts - flutes	struts - huts - its
let's - bets - moats	hats - closet - bats
knots - tots - kids	bites - sits - tights

- Tell a word that rhymes with *bats, floats, hoots, huts, knots, treats, waits, bets, baits, fights.*

Vocabulary Development

- Read the story and discuss vocabulary that may be new to students: *fleets, foghorns, newts, accessories, ingredients, plots, glitz, moat, trudge, struts, announces, unfazed, gloomy, wizardly, disrupted, tribe.*

- Point out and discuss figurative expressions: *back on track, Hall of Fame great.*

Associations

- Present pictures or real objects from the story and discuss who would use them.

- Play a guessing game. Have children guess who you are according to the objects you tell them you use.

Functions

- Present pictures or real objects from the story. Discuss the uses of the various objects found in the story.

- Put pictures or objects in a container. Take turns choosing an object or picture and telling its function so that someone else can guess what was chosen.

Multiple-Meaning Words

- Discuss words in the story that have multiple meanings: *stars, bats, blue, sinking, plate, scramble.*

Plurals

- Use the sequence cards or picture cards to elicit plural forms.

Critical Thinking

- As you read the book, cover the main pictures and have children predict what the characters will do with the various items they find in the closet. When using the full-color version of the storybook, you may use the small closet pictures with highlighted objects to cue children visually.

- Fill a box or bag with objects. Take turns choosing an object and thinking of something to do with the item. See how many creative uses individuals or groups can think of for an item.

Our Parade WITH 2 Blue Bikes

One day
we had a parade
with two blue bikes,
followed by
three ducks on trikes.

They balanced bricks
on long, black spikes
in our parade
with two blue bikes.

After ducks came
four big yaks
licking dripping
candle wax.

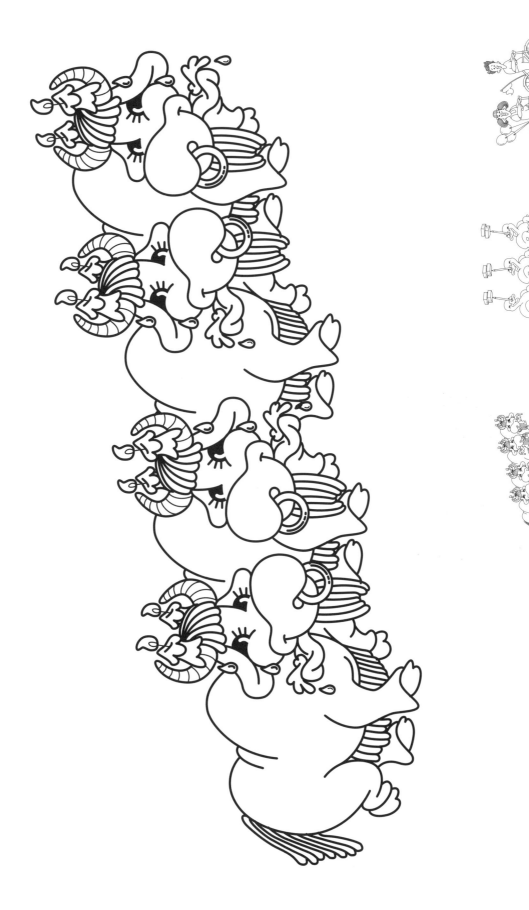

Five fire trucks
were next in line.
Red lights flashed
and the sirens whined.

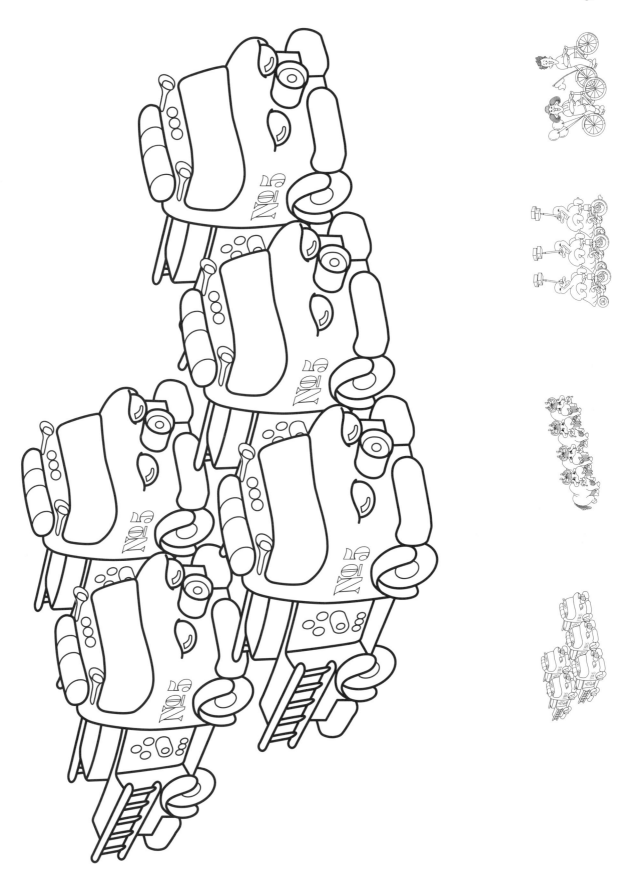

Six cooks
carried cakes
topped with gum
and frosted flakes.

Seven hens
with baby chicks
chirped behind
the cakes of six.

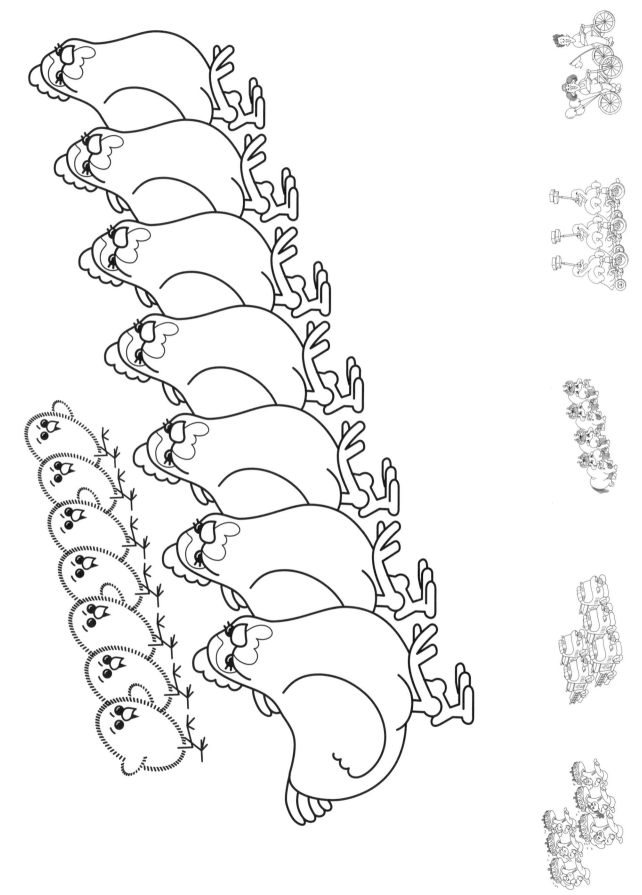

Eight emus followed
with high leg kicks
and fancy walks
behind the chicks.

Nine jacks
with ticking clocks
followed eight
emu walks
behind seven
hens and chicks
and cooks with cakes
(they carried six).
Four yaks licked wax,
three ducks rode trikes
in our parade
with two blue bikes.

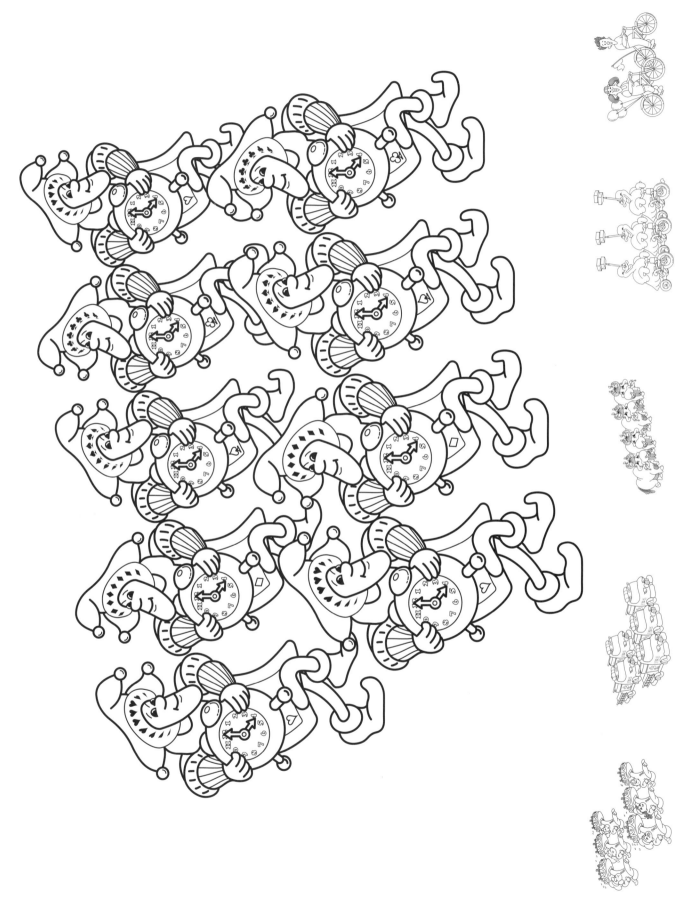

Ten snakes in back
started hissing
when they saw
fire trucks missing.
Alarms rang out
on nine jacks' clocks
that upset eight
emu walks
which startled seven
hens and chicks
that ran into
six cooks that tripped
four yaks that bumped
three ducks with spikes
in our parade
with two blue bikes.

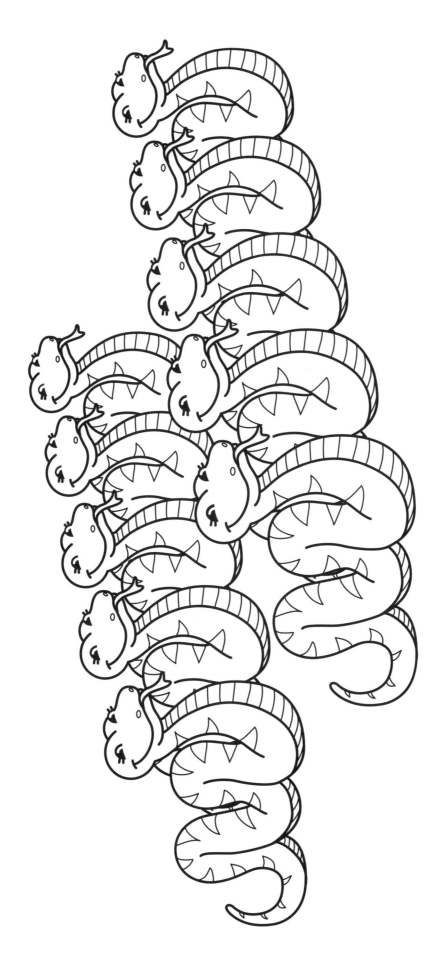

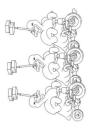

Amid the mix
of bikes and ducks
and yaks and cooks
and wax and clucks,
on top of emus,
clockless jacks
and snakes all piled
in the back,
we stood amazed
and uttered, "Yikes!"
at our parade
with two blue bikes.

Five fire trucks
came back in view.
"We didn't mean
to frighten you,
but we were needed
lickety-split
to douse a fire
on some sticks."

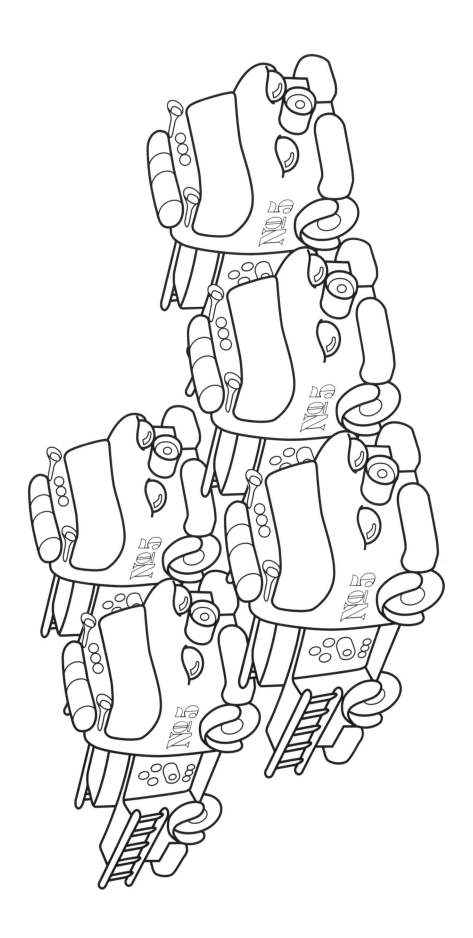

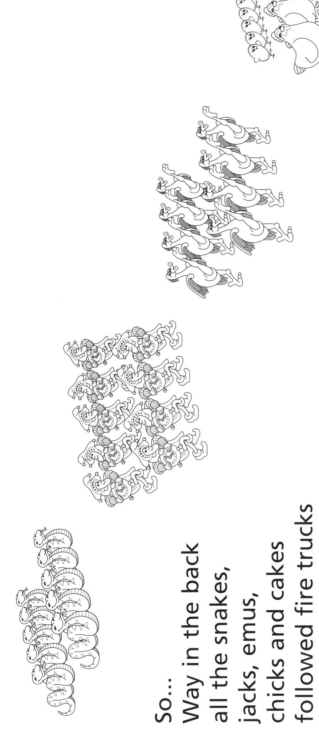

Four yaks went back
to licking wax,
three ducks lined up
with happy quacks.
A new parade was
on its way
led by two
blue bikes
one day.

So...
Way in the back
all the snakes,
jacks, emus,
chicks and cakes
followed fire trucks
returned
from putting out
the sticks that burned.

Sequence Cards

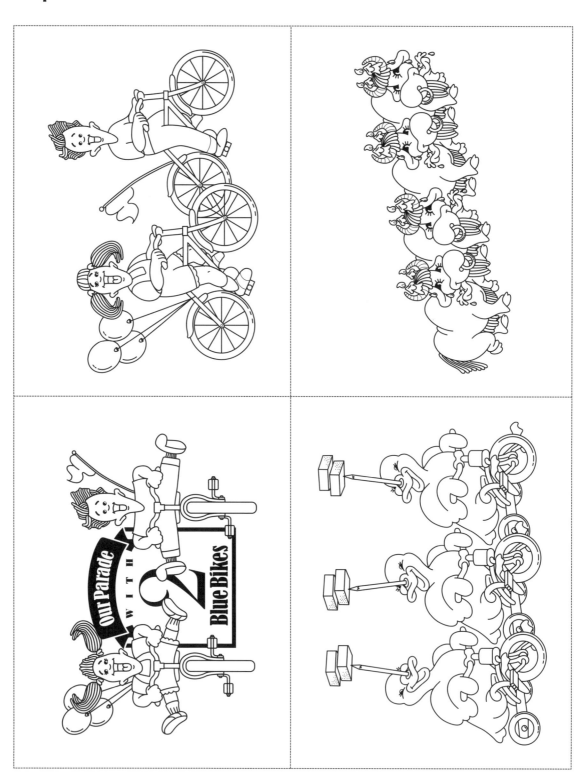

Sequence Cards

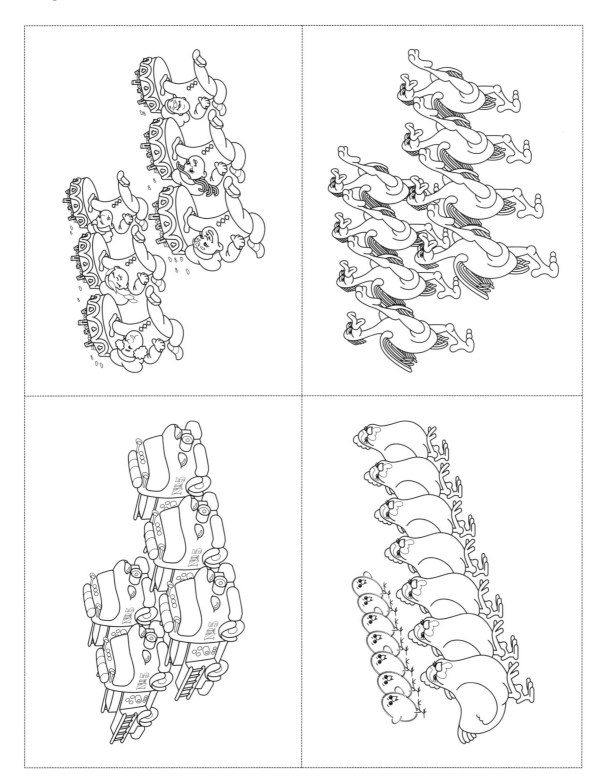

Sequence Cards

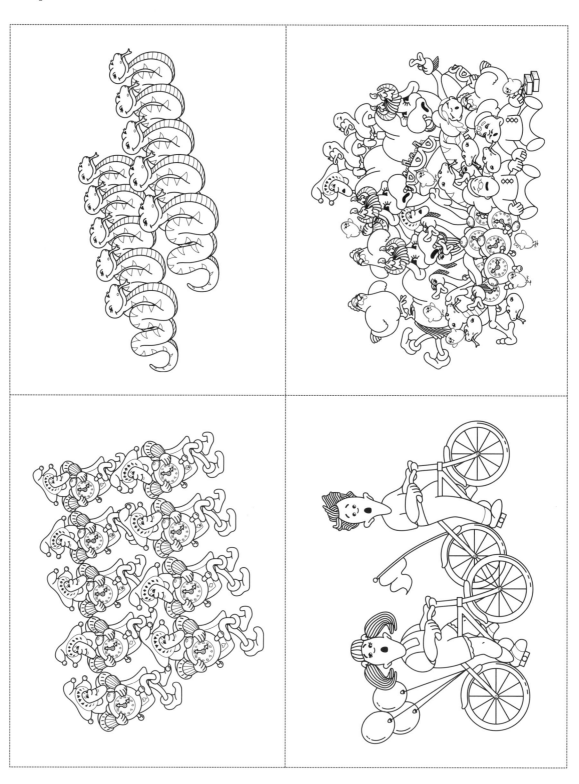

Picture Cards

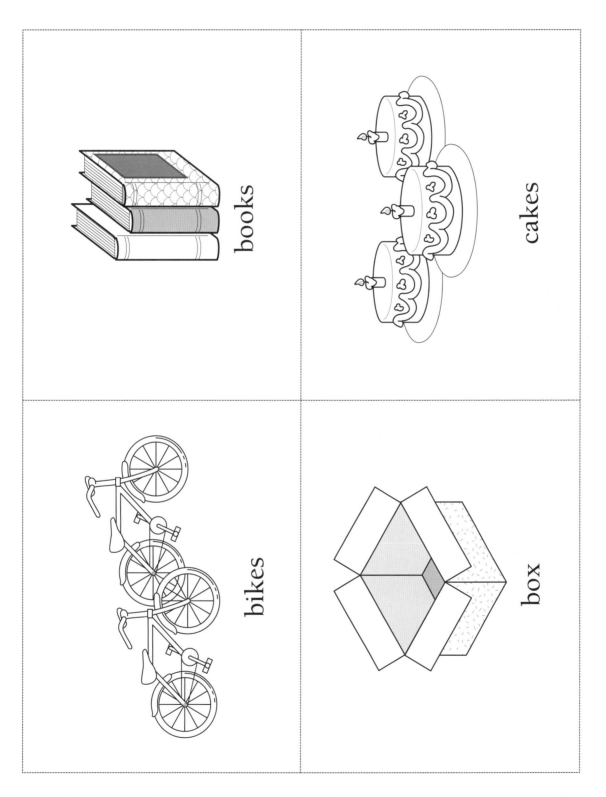

books

cakes

bikes

box

Picture Cards

clocks

ducks

chicks

cooks

Picture Cards

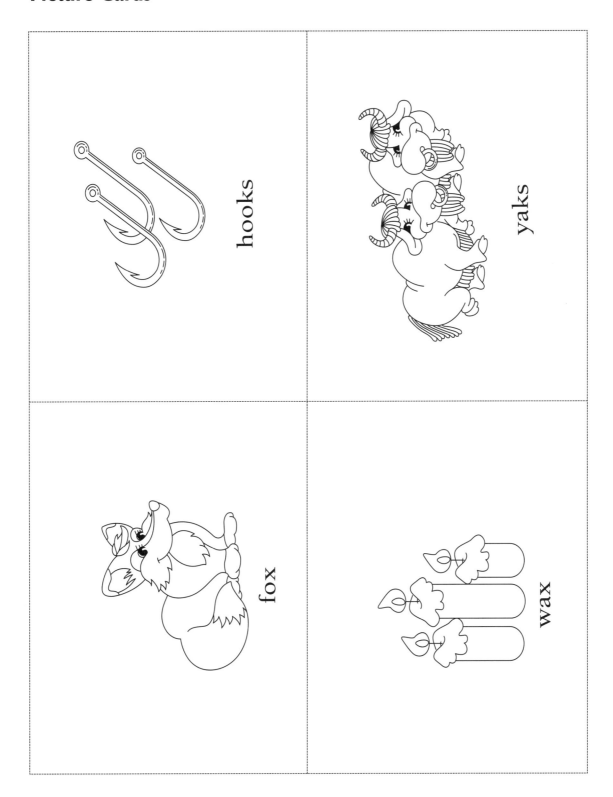

hooks

yaks

fox

wax

Word Count List

Final /ks/	
Word	Frequency
bikes	7
bricks	1
cakes	4
chicks	5
clocks	2
clucks	1
cooks	4
ducks	6
flakes	1
jacks	3
jacks'	1
kicks	1
mix	1
quacks	1
six	4
snakes	3
spikes	2
sticks	2
trikes	2
trucks	4
walks	3
wax	4
yaks	5
yikes	1

Total Words: 68

Picture Card List

Final /ks/
bikes
books
box
cakes
chicks
clocks
cooks
ducks
fox
hooks
wax
yaks

Production Practice and Carryover Activities

- Create new parades using the **final /ks/** sequence cards or individual student picture cards.

- Ride real **bikes** and **trikes** for a parade.

- Pretend you are **cooks** and bake **cakes**.

- Draw a **cakes** and glue frosted **flakes** on top.

- Have frosted **flakes** for **snacks**.

- Pretend you are emus doing high leg **kicks**. Use a die or a spinner to determine how many **kicks** each person should do.

- Play with fire **trucks**.

- Make **clocks** and use **sticks** (from trees or popsicles) to make the hands.

- Play Charades and pretend you are various animals from the story (**ducks, snakes, chicks**).

- Play the Memory game using the **jacks** from different card **decks**.

Extension Activities

Rhyming

- Do these words rhyme? (yes or no)

bikes - trikes	peeks - cheeks
cakes - cooks	red - rakes
clocks - box	yaks - wax
snakes - flakes	quacks - night
chicks - hens	ducks - clucks

- Which words rhyme?

bikes - cakes - yikes	necks - checks - red
chicks - clocks - box	hens - clucks - ducks
cooks - books - bird	snakes - flakes - candles
sticks - trucks - fix	jacks - quacks - kicks
sneaks - water - beaks	wax - cooks - books

- Tell a word that rhymes with *sticks, ducks, jacks, bikes, wax, walks, snakes, cooks, peeks, pecks.*

Vocabulary Development

- Read the story and discuss vocabulary that may be new to students: *amazed, balanced, chirped, douse, emus, hissing, jacks, lickety-split, sirens, startled, wax, whine, yaks.*

Absurdities

- Present individual sequence cards and talk to students about the absurdities in the pictures. *Can ducks really ride tricycles? How do ducks really move? Who rides tricycles? Do we frost cakes with gum and frosted flakes? What would you use to frost a cake?*

Plurals

- Use the sequence cards or picture cards to elicit plural forms.

Sequencing

- Give simple directions for children to sequence the picture cards to form a new parade. For younger children, use only two or three pictures. Increase the number of pictures according to individual ability levels. Use terms such as *first, second, next,* and *last* to tell the sequence. Allow children to create their own parade sequence and explain it to you using the same terms.

Critical Thinking

- Review the segment of the story where the fire trucks are missing and the reason the trucks were gone. Sequence the picture cards and remove individual pictures. Have children think of reasons why characters on each card could have left in the story (e.g., *The ducks decided to go take a swim* or *The cooks needed to do the dishes*).

The lions, the leopards
and the brown kangaroo,
the hippos, the rhinos,
the whole beastly crew,
are all getting ready
by quarter past two
for the Big Leapin' Lizards'
Zoo Hullabaloo.

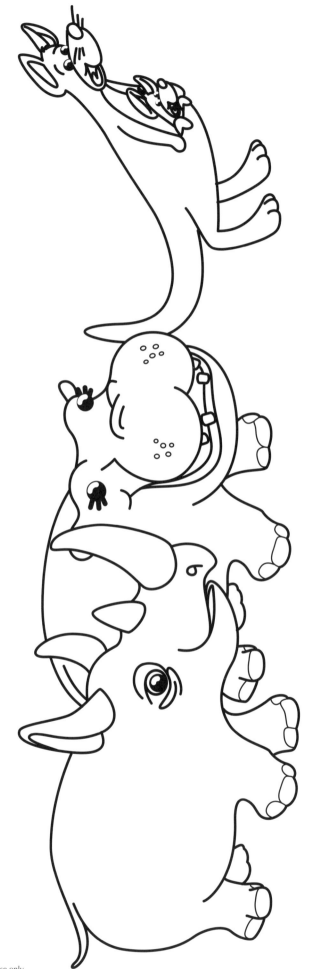

The peacocks arrive
with flourish and flash.
Their fine feather plumes
are a colorful splash.

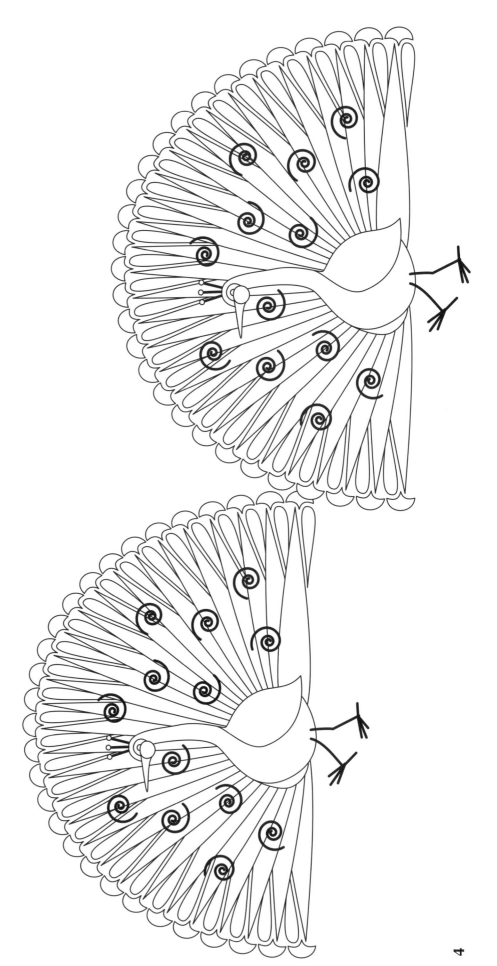

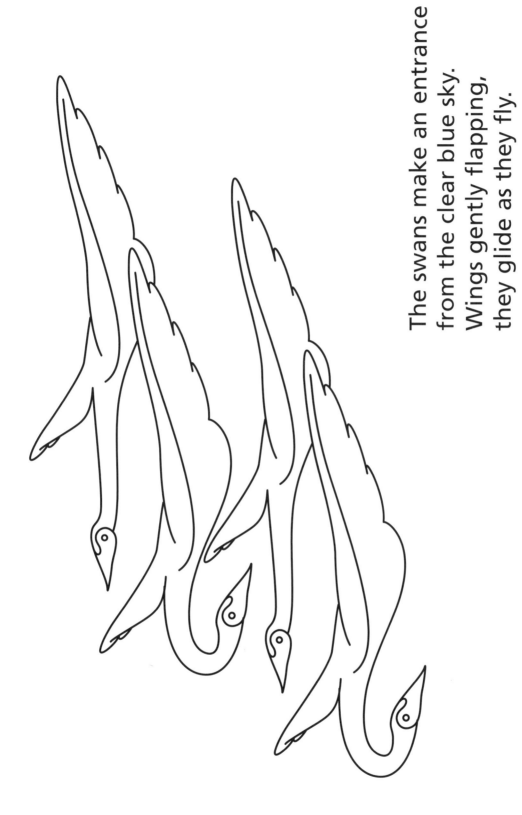

The swans make an entrance
from the clear blue sky.
Wings gently flapping,
they glide as they fly.

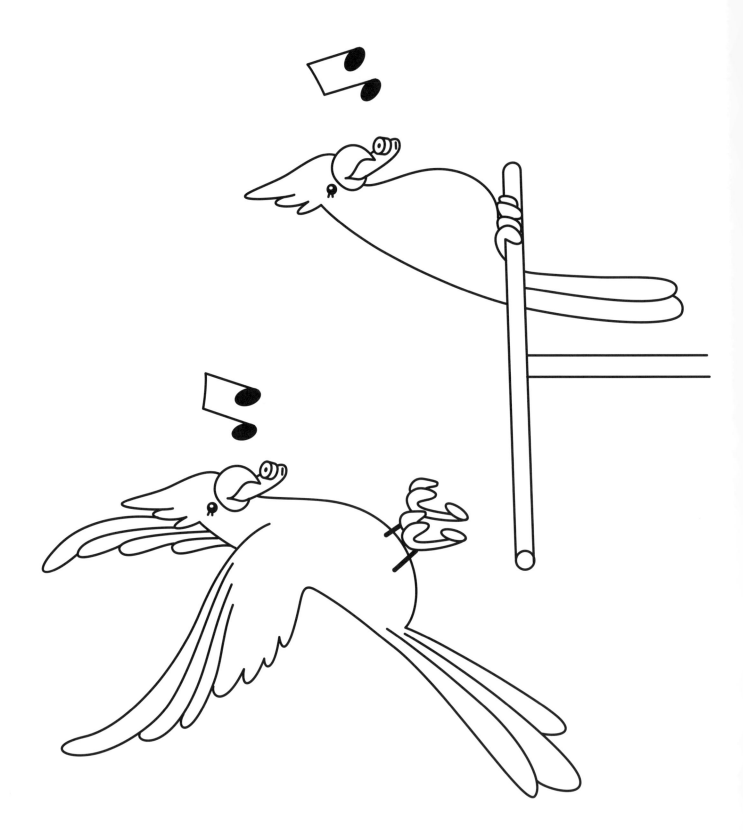

The animals clap
at the white cockatoos.
They loop in and land
while blowing kazoos.

Soon every bird,
every ostrich and emu
are at Leapin' Lizards'
Zoo Hullabaloo.

A fabulous lunch
fills a huge room.
Ten tables stand
with lilies in bloom.

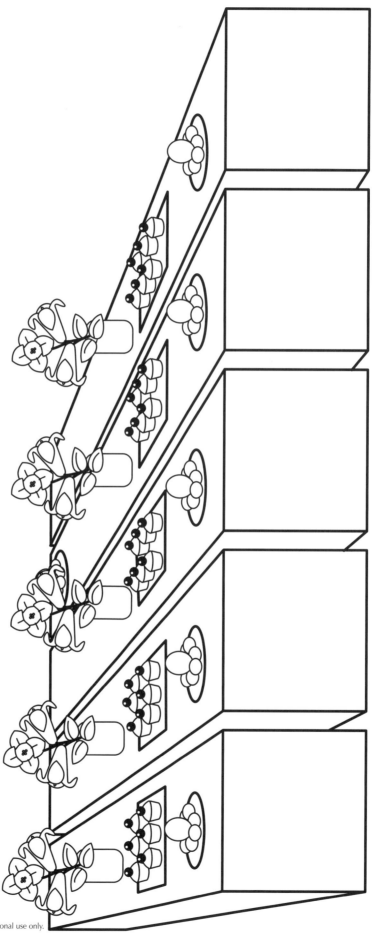

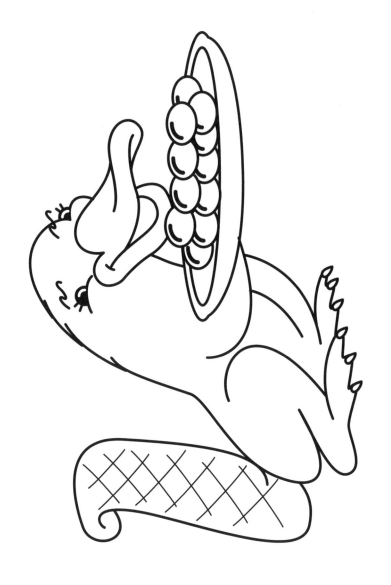

Platypus brings
a big plate of plums,
pickled and plenty
for his animal chums.

The flamingos' dessert
has a fruit-flavored touch,
and...

...llamas' lollies are licked
and loved very much!

The dishes are endless
—such big bowls of stew—
at the Big Leapin' Lizards'
Zoo Hullabaloo.

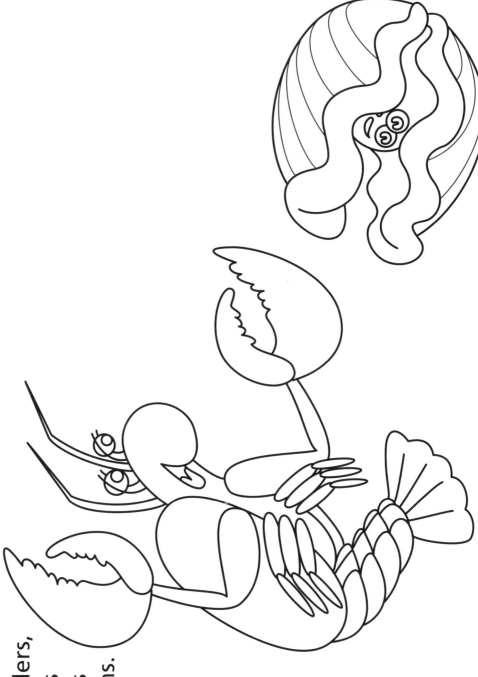

Some of the animals
gladly play songs
for long-legged dancing
and song sing-alongs.

The lobsters, flounders,
sea slugs, and clams
lay down some licks
and jam groovy jams.

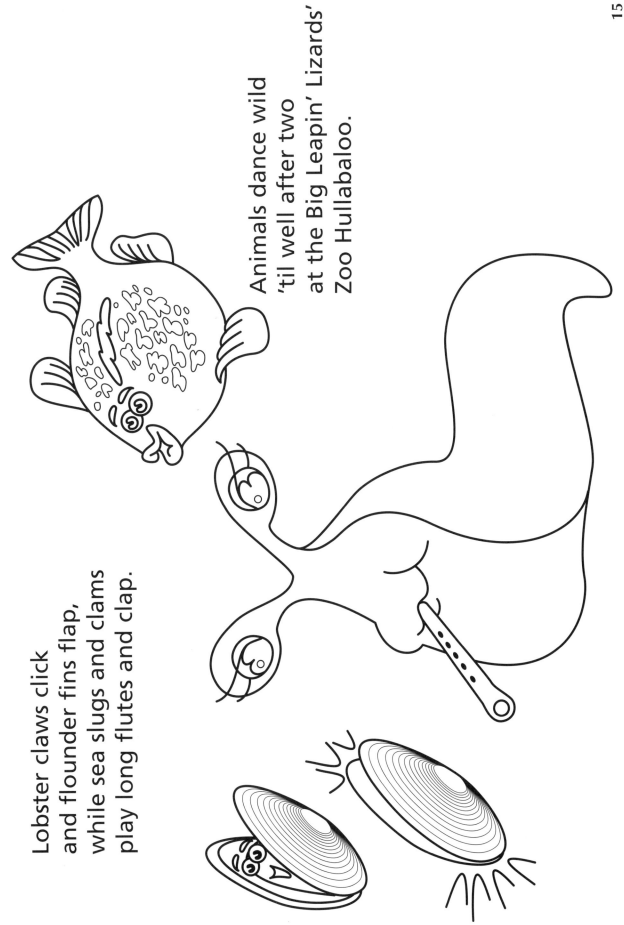

Animals dance wild
'til well after two
at the Big Leapin' Lizards'
Zoo Hullabaloo.

Lobster claws click
and flounder fins flap,
while sea slugs and clams
play long flutes and clap.

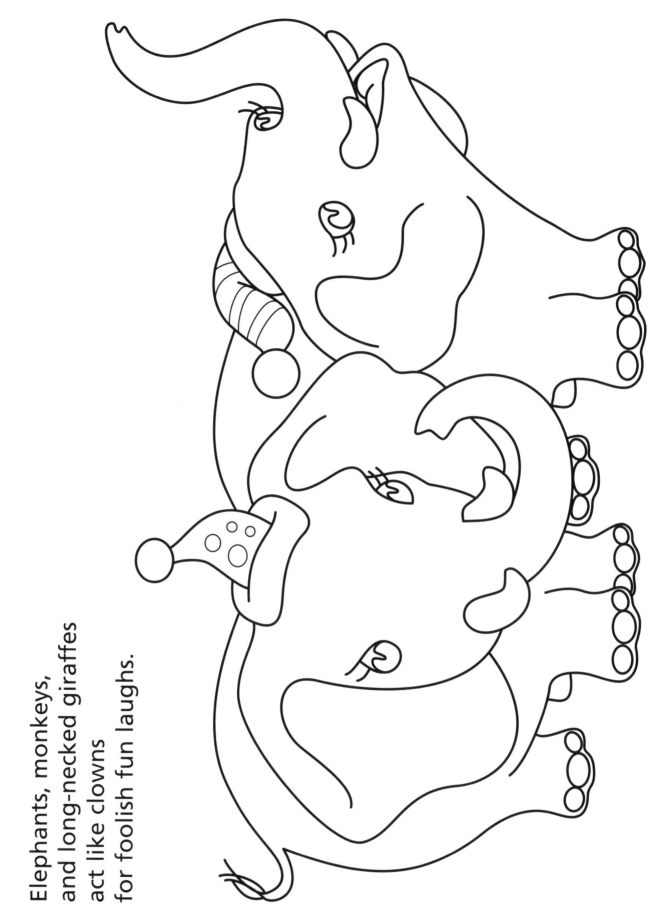

Elephants, monkeys,
and long-necked giraffes
act like clowns
for foolish fun laughs.

One elephant lifts
her trunk with a wail,
and a wild monkey clings
to the end with his tail.

The monkeys flip up
and fling with a flair,
and land on the necks
of giraffes lined up there.

Everyone giggles
with glee at the view,
this Big Leapin' Lizards'
Zoo Hullabaloo.

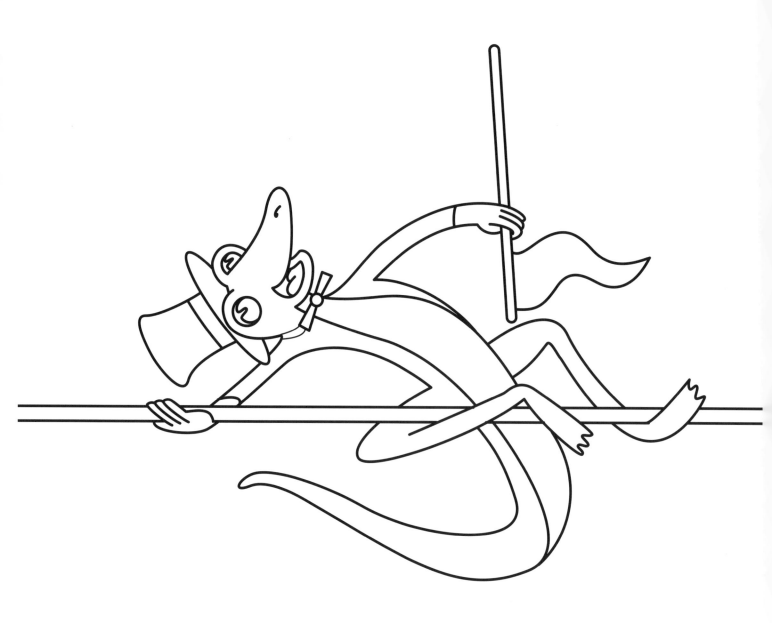

Leapin' Lizards
at last take the stage,
sliding down poles
while waving blue flags.

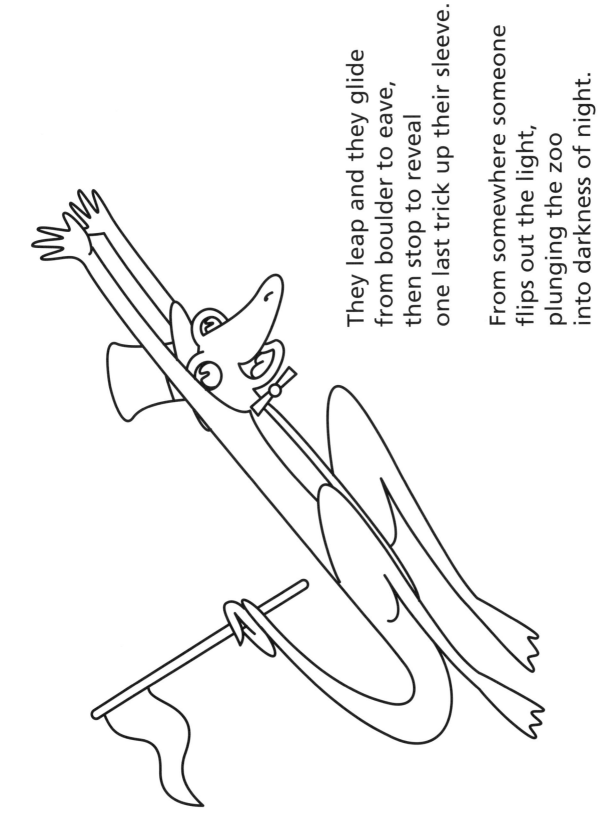

They leap and they glide
from boulder to eave,
then stop to reveal
one last trick up their sleeve.

From somewhere someone
flips out the light,
plunging the zoo
into darkness of night.

When lights come back on
a spotlight has lit
the biggest fudge sundae
made on the planet.

Lots of sweet chocolate
lumped high on ice cream—
enough to feed all;
a dessert-lover's dream!

The surrounding slices
of lemon and lime
make this final course
a treat for all time.

"Please help yourself,"
say both Leapin' Lizards.
"Take all you want!
Stuff all your gizzards!"

"It's our way to thank you
and wish you the best.
But before you dig in,
there's one last request."

"Let loose a yell
that's heard through the zoo
for the Big Leapin' Lizards'
Zoo Hullabaloo!"

24

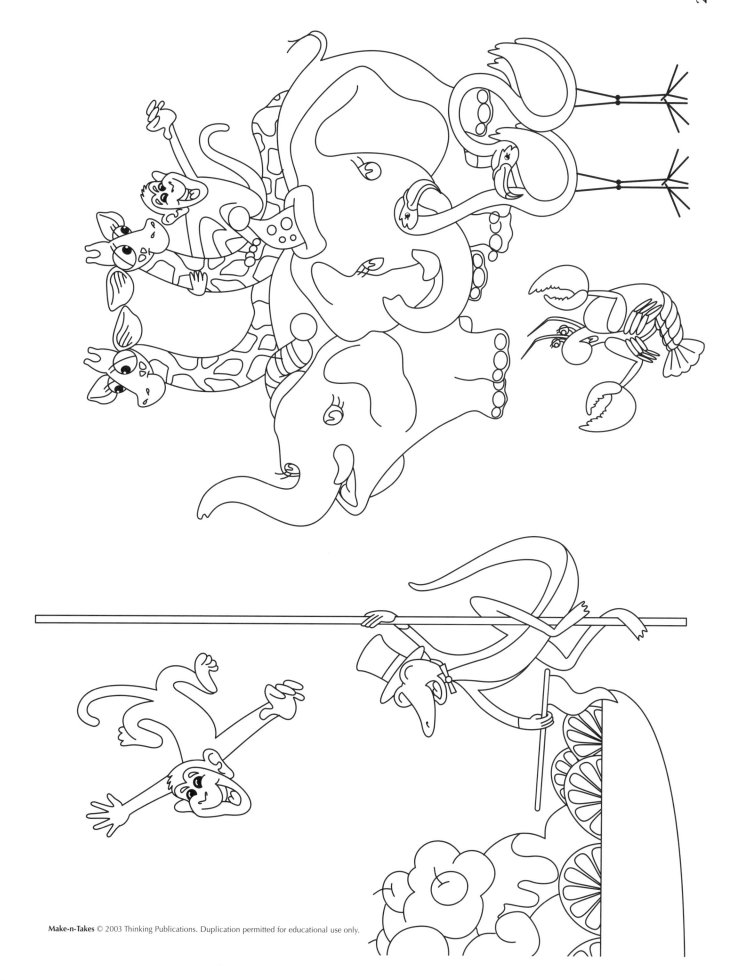

Sequence Cards

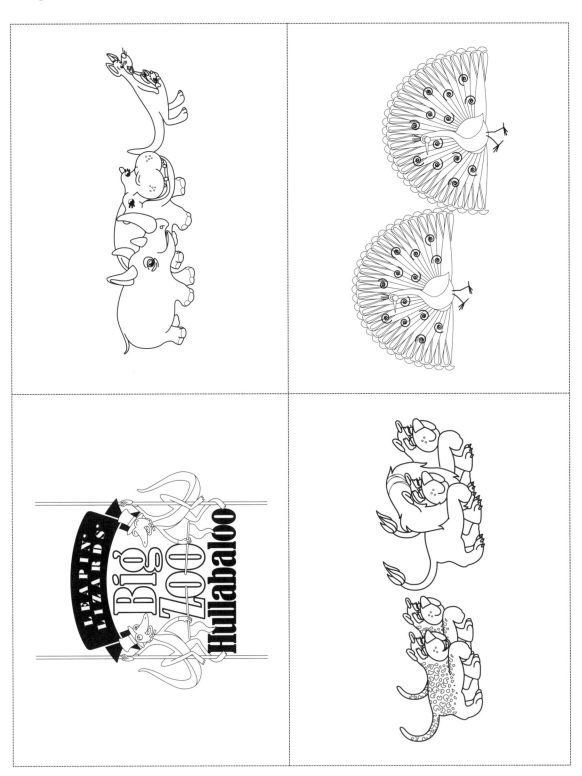

Sequence Cards

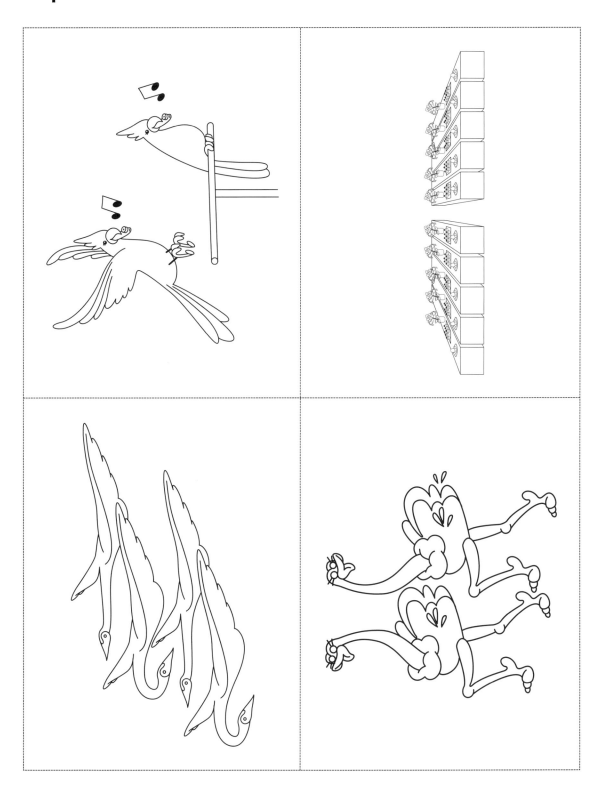

Sequence Cards

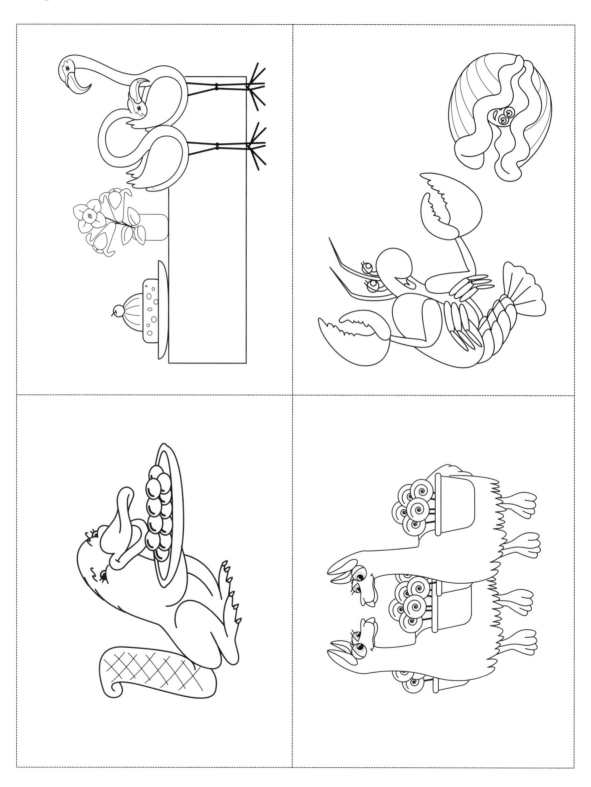

Sequence Cards

Sequence Cards

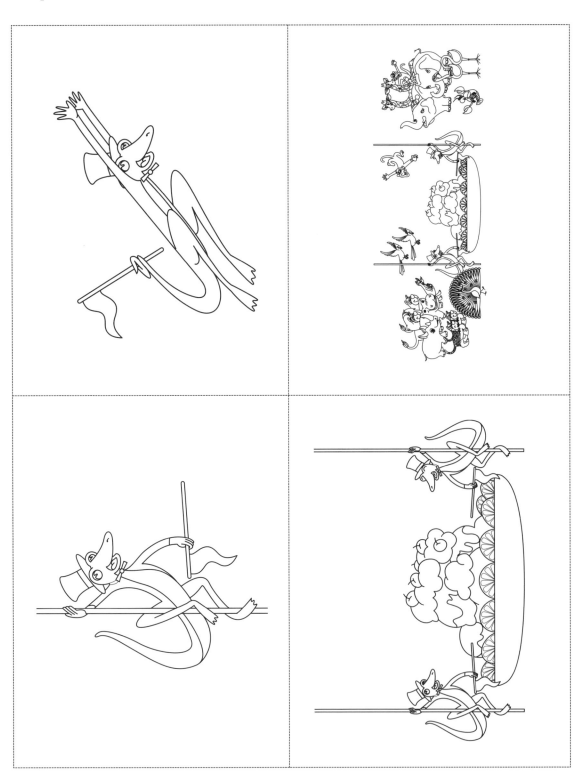

Picture Cards

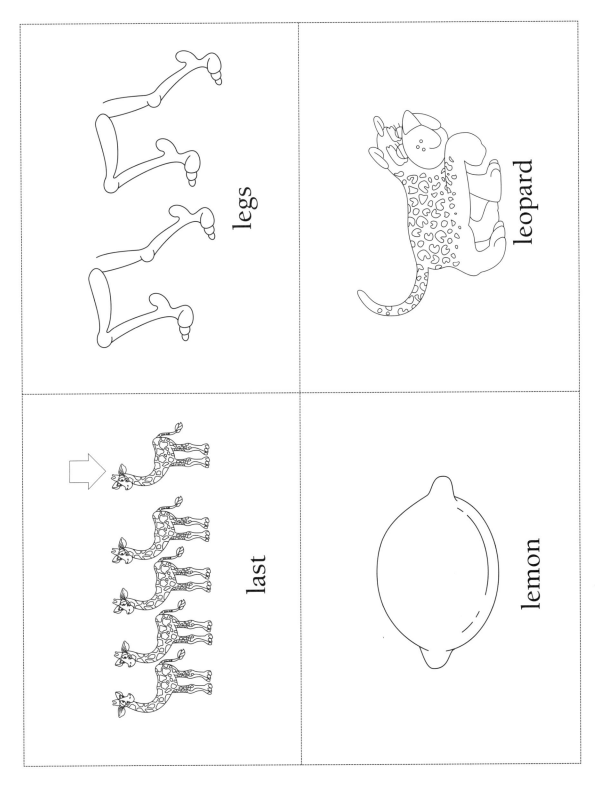

legs

leopard

last

lemon

Picture Cards

light

lion

lick

lilies

Picture Cards

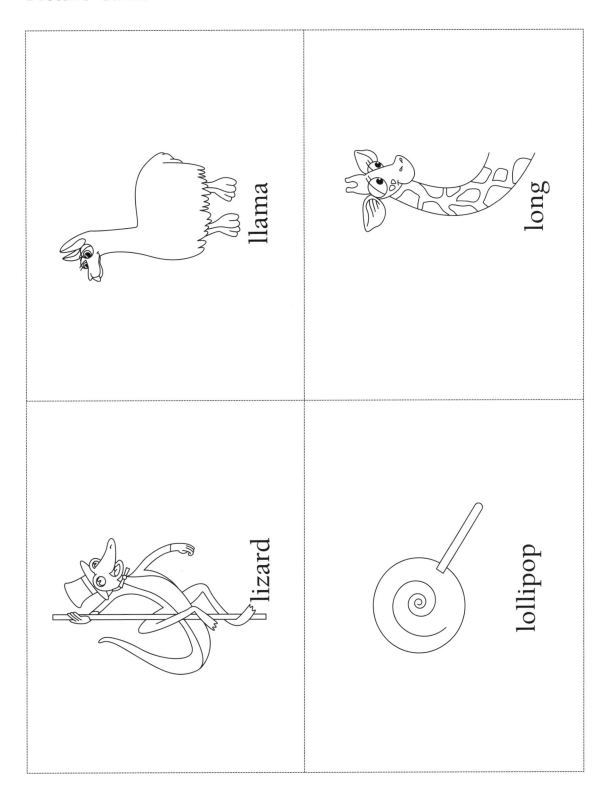

llama

long

lizard

lollipop

Picture Cards

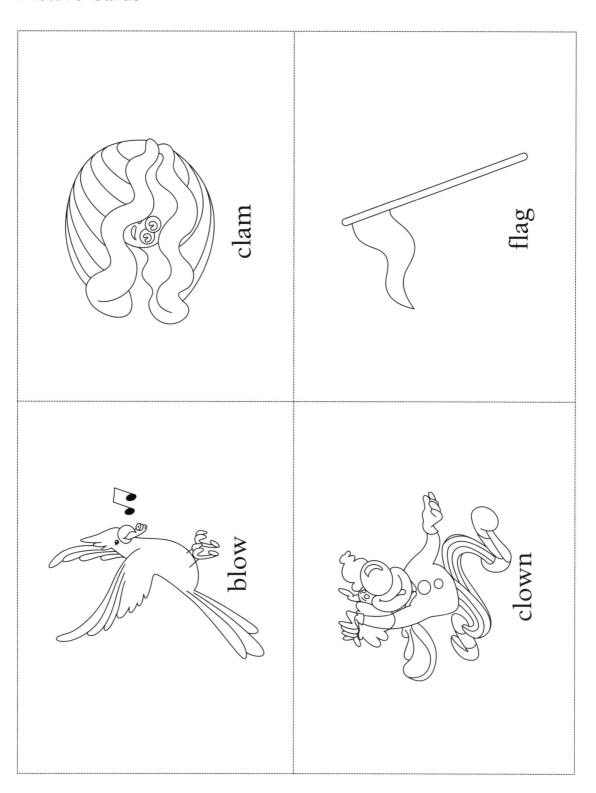

clam

flag

blow

clown

Picture Cards

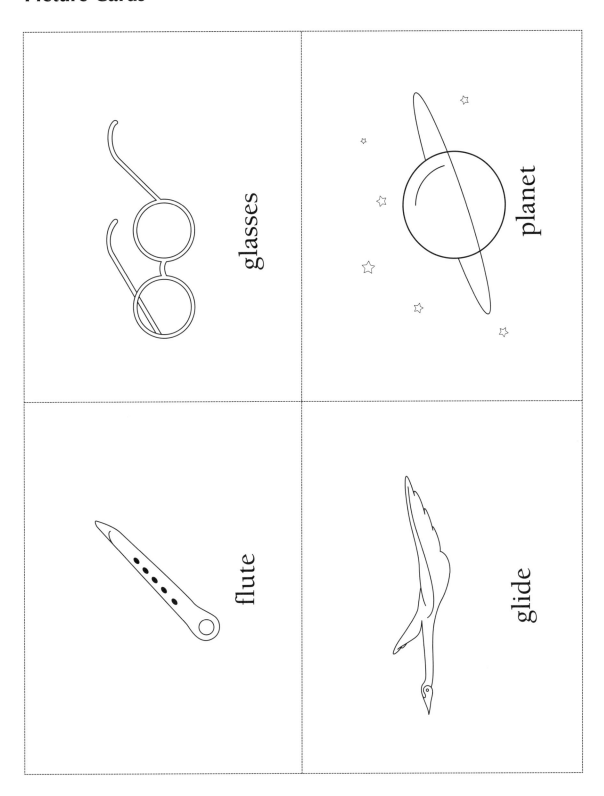

glasses

planet

flute

glide

Picture Cards

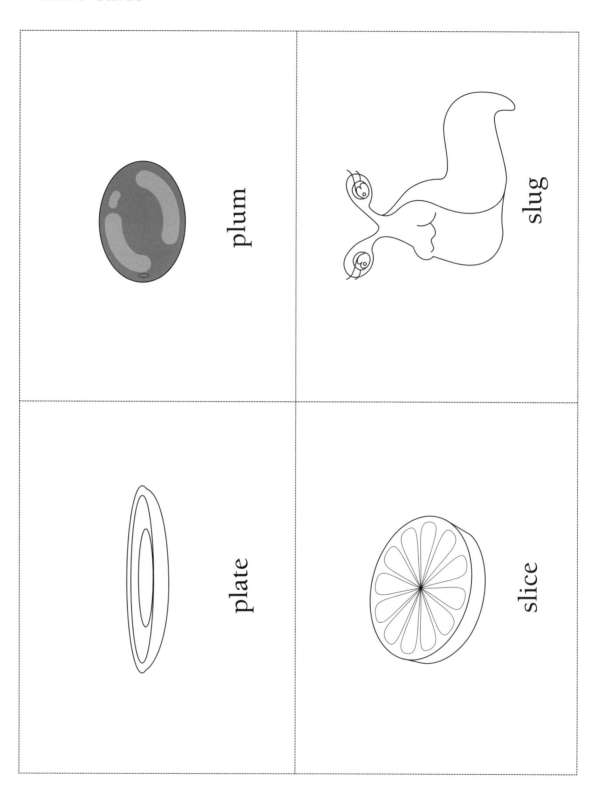

plum

slug

plate

slice

Word Count Lists

Initial /l/		Initial /l/ Clusters	
Word	Frequency	Word	Frequency
land	2	bloom	1
last	3	blowing	1
laughs	1	blue	2
lay	1	clams	2
leap	1	clap	2
Leapin'	8	claws	1
legged	1	clear	1
lemon	1	click	1
leopards	1	clings	1
let	1	clowns	1
licked	1	flags	1
licks	1	flair	1
lifts	1	flamingos'	1
light	1	flap	1
lights	1	flapping	1
like	1	flash	1
lilies	1	flavored	1
lime	1	fling	1
lined	1	flip	1
lions	1	flips	1
lit	1	flounder	1
Lizards	2	flounders	1
Lizards'	6	flourish	1
llamas	1	flutes	1
lobster	1	fly	1
lobsters	1	gladly	1
lollies	1	glee	1
long	3	glide	2
loop	1	planet	1
loose	1	plate	1
lots	1	Platypus	1
loved	1	play	1
lover's	1	please	1
lumped	1	plenty	1
lunch	1	plumes	1
		plums	1
		plunging	1
		sleeve	1
		slices	1
		sliding	1
		slugs	2
Total Words: 53		**Total Words: 46**	

Picture Card Lists

Initial /l/

last
legs
lemon
leopard
lick
light
lilies
lion
lizard
llama
lollipop
long

Initial /l/ Clusters

blow
clam
clown
flag
flute
glasses
glide
planet
plate
plum
slice
slug

Production Practice and Carryover Activities

- Create a path with target /l/ and /l/ cluster picture cards. **Leap** to each picture and say its name.

- Make a straight **line** with pictures. Take turns **leaping** as far as possible and name the picture you are next to when you **land**.

- Use picture cards or objects to make a **long line**. Talk about which picture or object is **last** in the **line**. Make more than one **line** and compare which is **longer**.

- Squeeze **lemons** and make **lemonade**. Pour the **lemonade** into **glasses**.

- **Lick lollipops.**

- Make **lunch.** Serve the food on **plates** and pour the drinks in **glasses**.

- **Glue** pictures of food on a paper **plate**.

- **Blow** kazoos, pinwheels, bubbles, or pieces of **plastic.**

- Act out an animal from the story. **Clap** after each performance.

- Make **blue** or **black flags.** Decorate them with **glue** and **glitter.**

Extension Activities

Rhyming

- Do these words rhyme? (yes or no)

land - line	plate - late
lime - dime	plum - come
lick - kick	glee - bloom
flip - flap	slice - dice
flags - bags	laugh - giraffe

- Which words rhyme?

lime - time - fly	loop - long - song
loose - bunch - lunch	plate - sleeve - mate
flutes - last - boots	slugs - bugs - slush
clap - claws - draws	leaping - flash - dash
sloth - flag - moth	lily - hilly - flower

- Tell a word that rhymes with *leap, bloom, flair, play, slide, lick, leg, land, blow, clown.*

Vocabulary Development

- Read the story and discuss vocabulary that may be new to students: *hullabaloo, crew, chums, eave, emu, flamingo, flounders, llamas, slugs, boulder, final course, flair, flourish, glee, request, cling, fling, reveal, view, wail.*

- Point out and discuss figurative expressions: *flips out all the lights, stuff your gizzards, make an entrance, started to jam, lay down some licks, one last trick up their sleeve, dig in.*

Attributes

- Present pictures of the various animals in the storybook (or use the sequence cards) to discuss their attributes. Identify unique characteristics. Take turns guessing animals according to someone's description of them.

Classification

- Group animals according to common characteristics (e.g., where they live, how they move, or specific number of body parts).

Plurals

- Use the sequence cards or picture cards to elicit plural forms.

Possessives

- Use the storybook illustrations or sequence cards to talk about items and who their owners are. Elicit various possessive forms with models and direct questions. For example, *The cockatoo brought a kazoo. Whose kazoo is it?* (the cockatoo's) or *The llama has lollipops. Whose lollipops are they?* (the llama's).

Critical Thinking

- Plan a hullabaloo (party). Brainstorm the details that need to be decided (e.g., what to celebrate, who to invite, when and where to have it, refreshments, and activities). Determine when things need to be done to be ready for the big event. Talk about what will happen if the various jobs aren't done on time or at all. Assign responsibilities.

- After an event occurs, evaluate how everything went. For example, ask *What things were done well? What things could have been better? How would you change things the next time we do this?*

Train, Truck, & Tractor

Train, Truck, and Tractor
were creating a scene.
They just couldn't agree
who was the better machine.

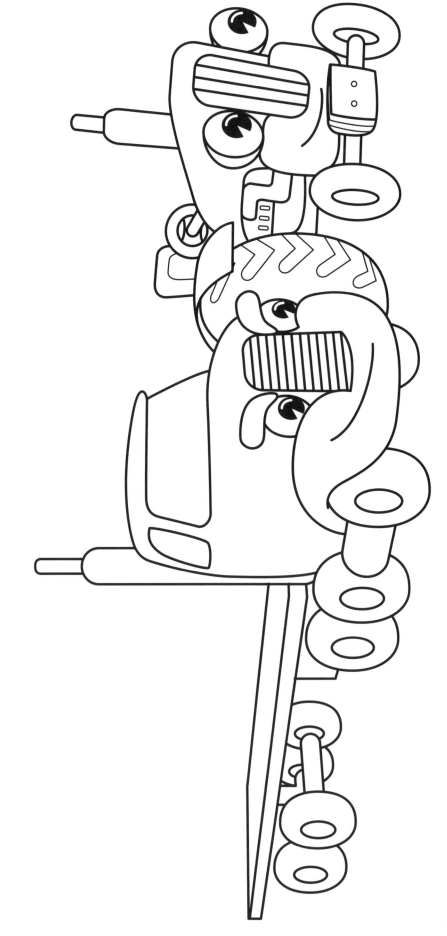

"My speed is unmatched,
my wheels never rest,"
Train boldly bragged.
"Trains are the best!"

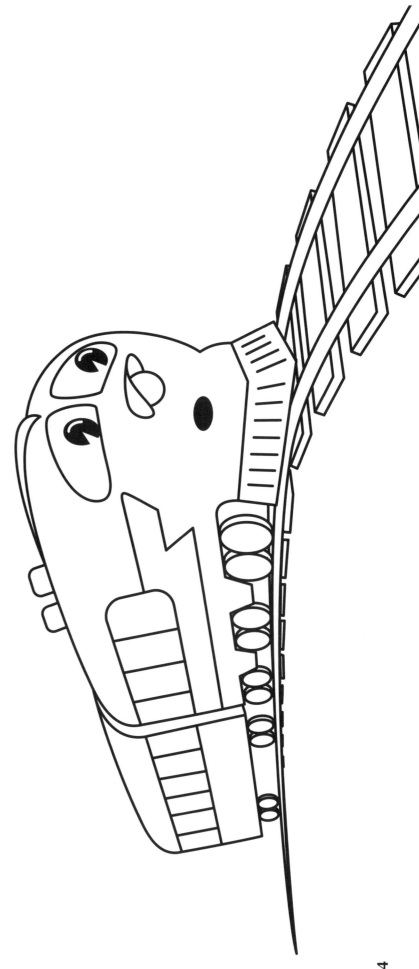

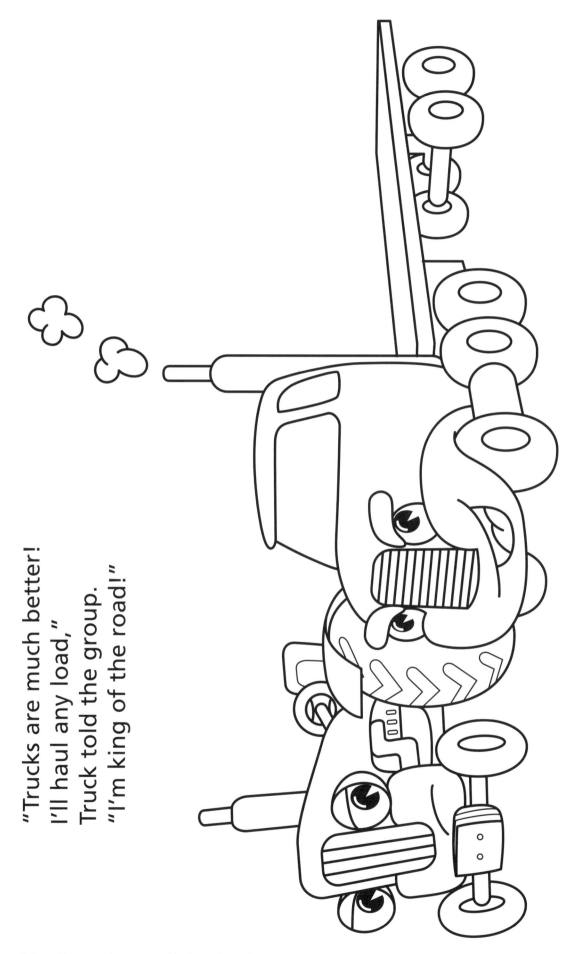

"Trucks are much better!
I'll haul any load,"
Truck told the group.
"I'm king of the road!"

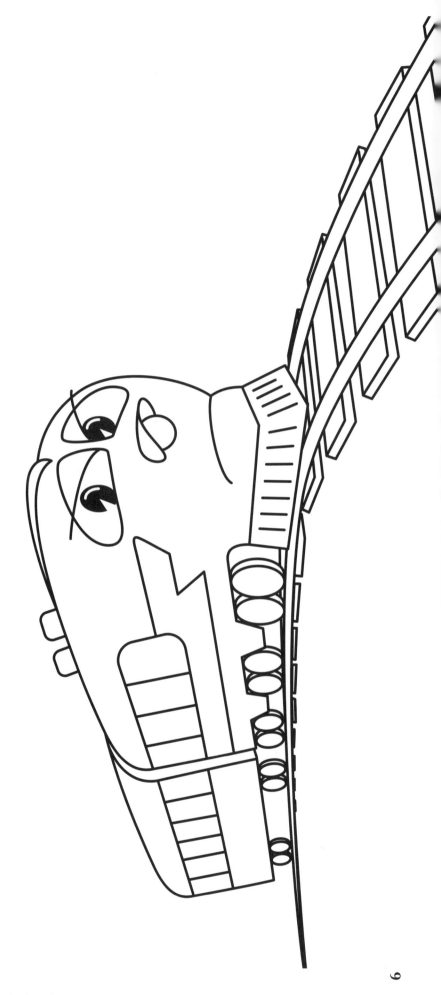

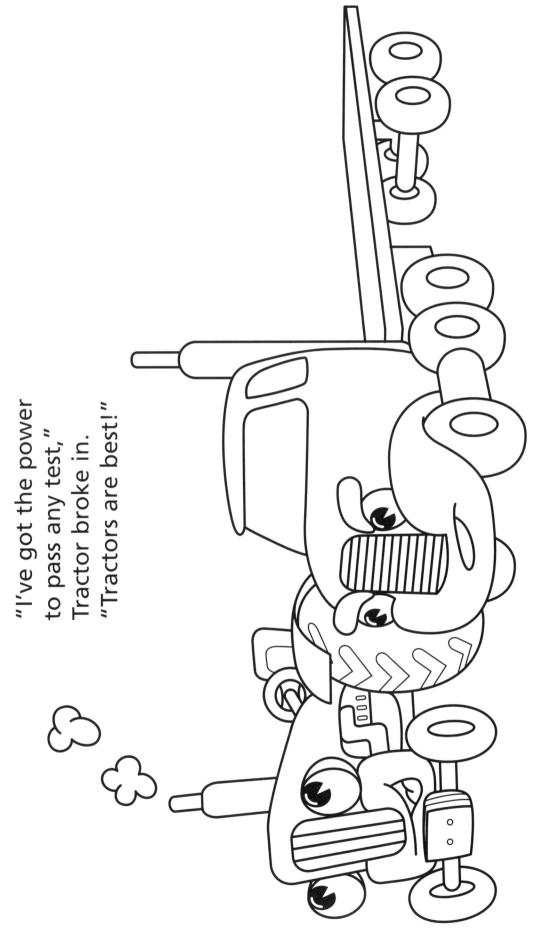

"I've got the power to pass any test,"
Tractor broke in.
"Tractors are best!"

"Let's have a race,
for our claims are in vain.
We'll find out who's right,"
suggested the train.

8

"Great idea!" Truck and Tractor agreed. "We'll start by the creek at quarter past three."

The train, the truck,
and the tractor machine
roared off the start.
Oh, what a scene!

The first one to cross
the old river bridge
would be awarded the
prize up on the ridge.

Train jumped out
in front right away.
It seemed clear to him
that he'd win the day.

"My speed is unmatched,
my wheels never rest.
I'll win the prize
'cause trains are the best!"

But problems arose
when the train tracks ran out.
Train had to stop
to grumble and pout.

Truck came along
and pulled up beside.
"Crawl on board, good friend,
I'll give you a ride."

"Trucks are much better!
I'll carry your load.
The trophy is mine.
I'm king of the road!"

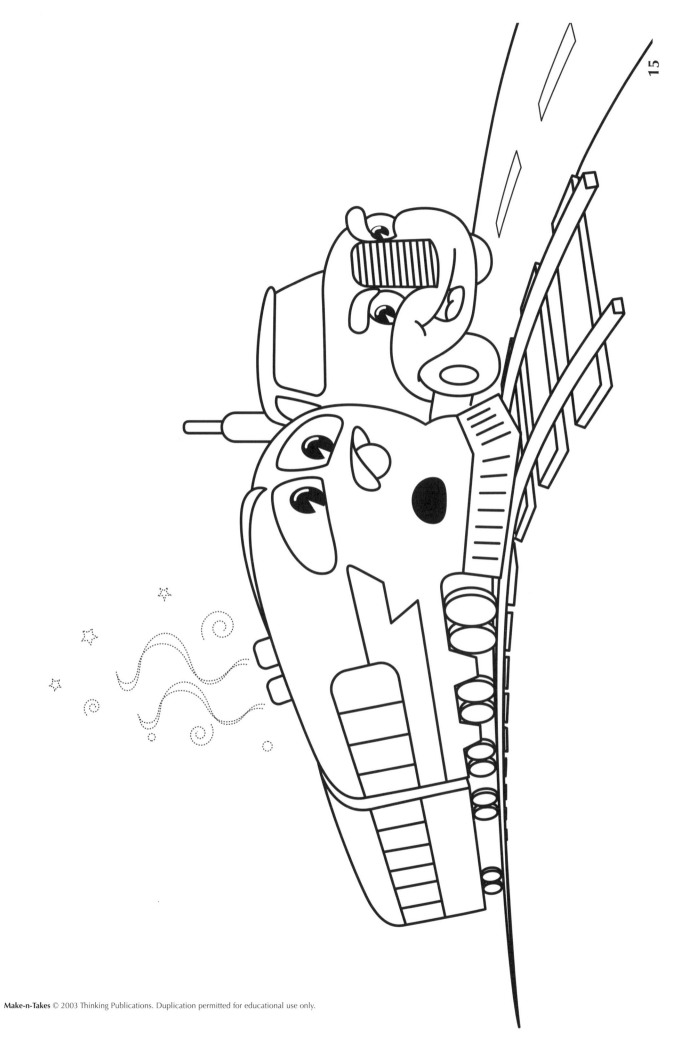

But the road on which Truck
and Train tried to travel
soon turned to mud
and sticky, black gravel.

As they stood trapped
in the gooey, black muck,
Tractor creeped up
to the train and the truck.

"There's power to spare
inside of my chest.
I'll pull you both out
'cause tractors are best!"

As Tractor's big wheels
ground through the slime,
he pried them both free
in a very short time.

Tractor pulled them so hard
he ran out of gas!
Now all three sat stopped
by that sticky, black mass.

So the three friends
soon came to realize
that no one deserved
the best-machine prize.

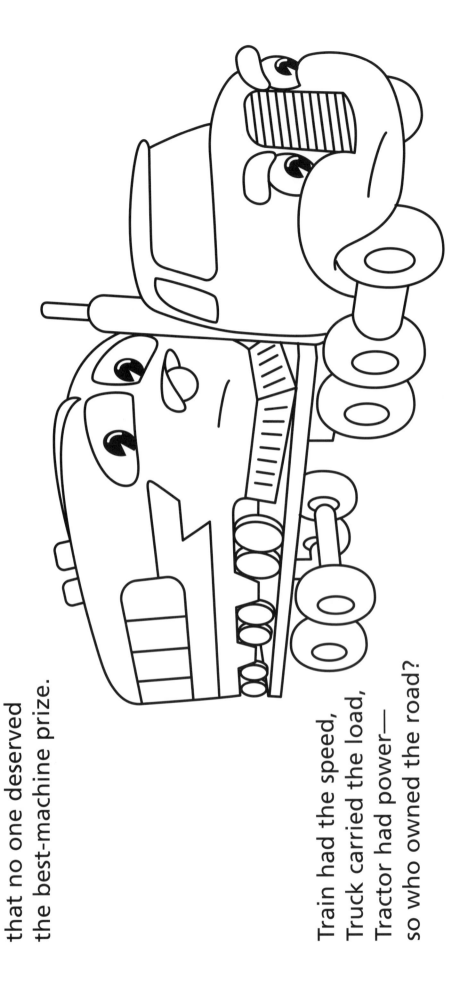

Train had the speed,
Truck carried the load,
Tractor had power—
so who owned the road?

All were special
in the traits they possessed.
And all had a chance
to show off their best.

24

So...
The three friends decided
they'd all won the race.
They all crossed together
and all claimed first place!

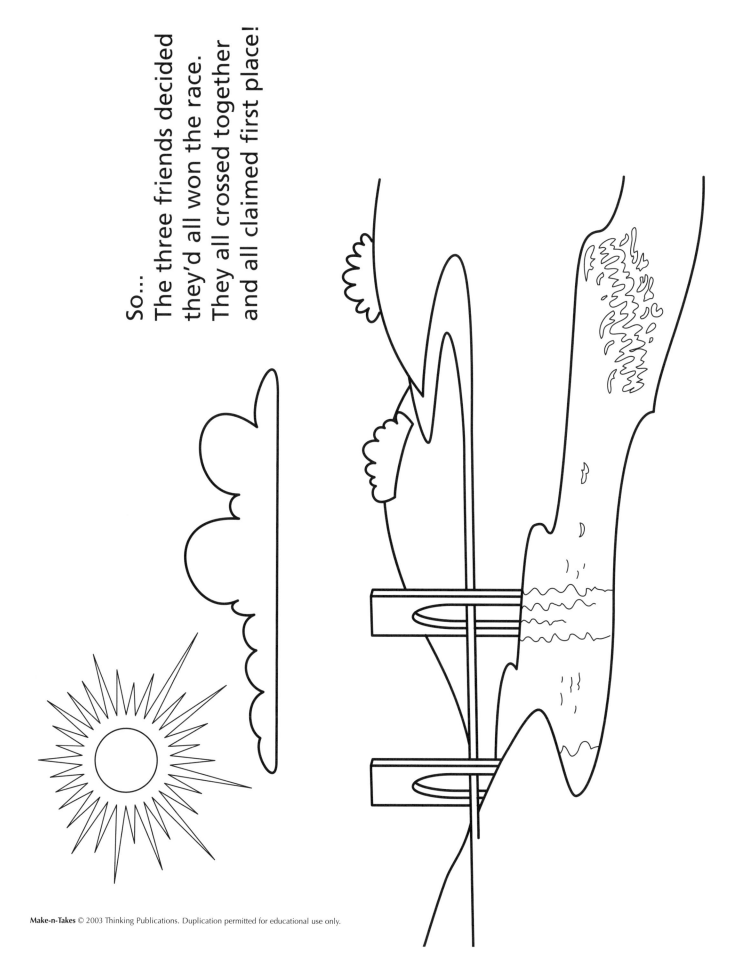

Sequence Cards

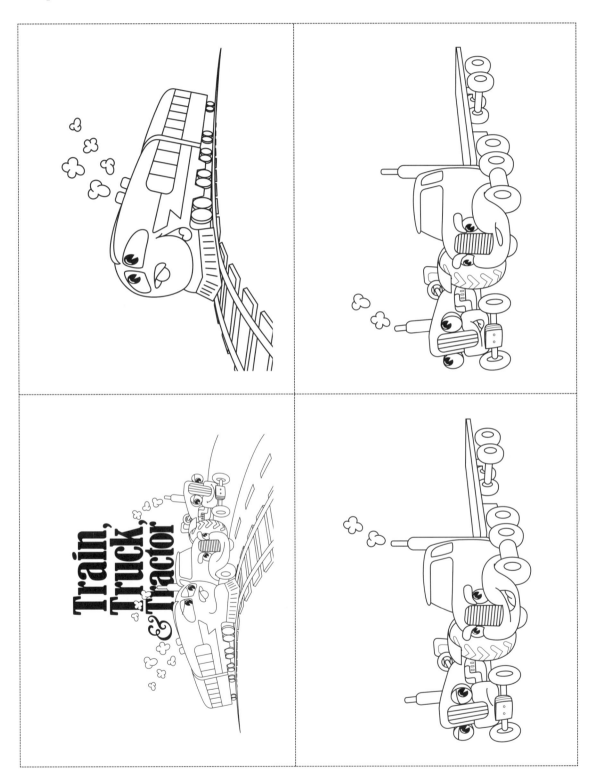

Sequence Cards

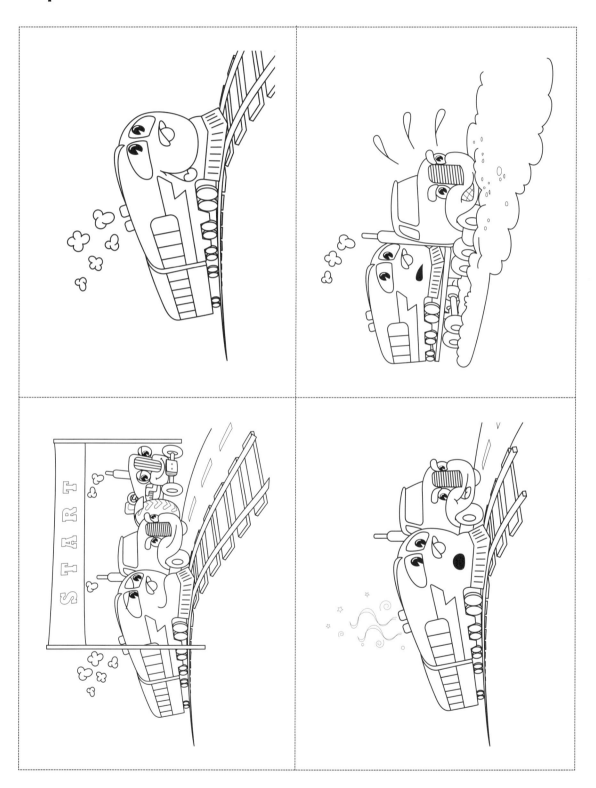

Sequence Cards

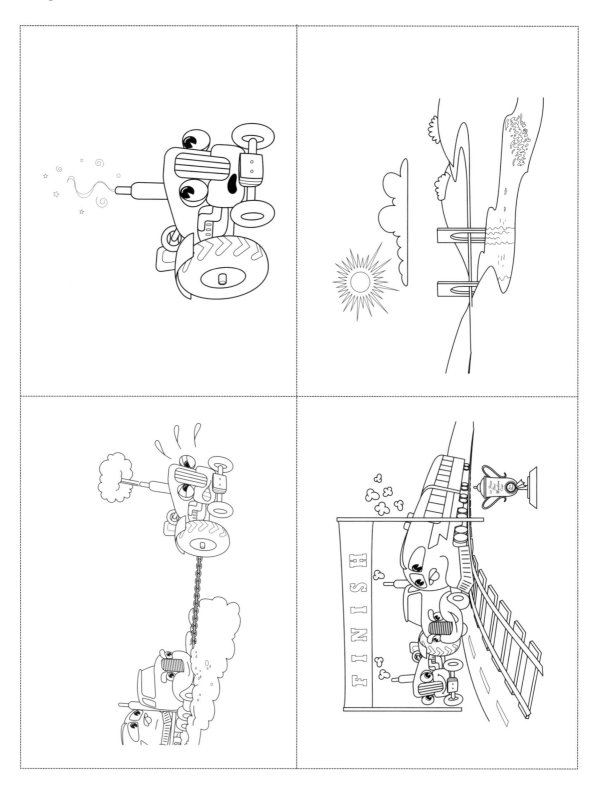

Picture Cards

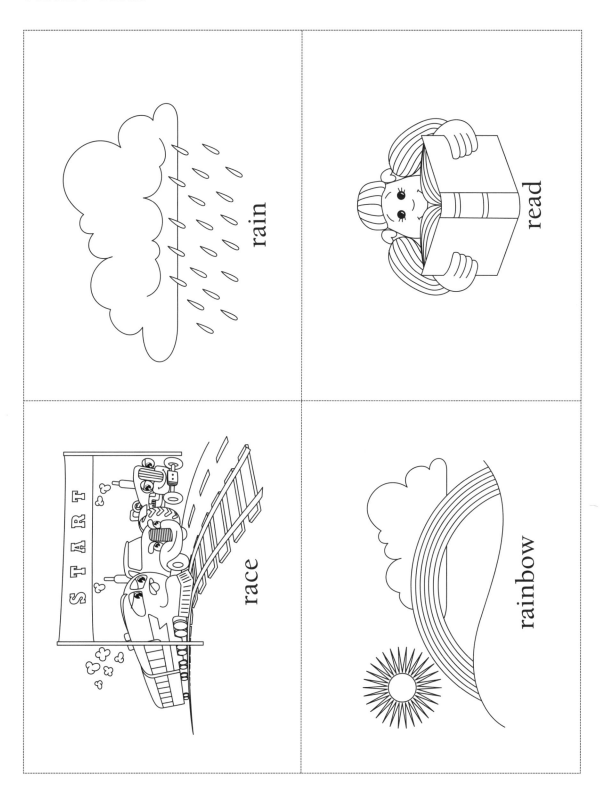

rain

read

race

rainbow

Picture Cards

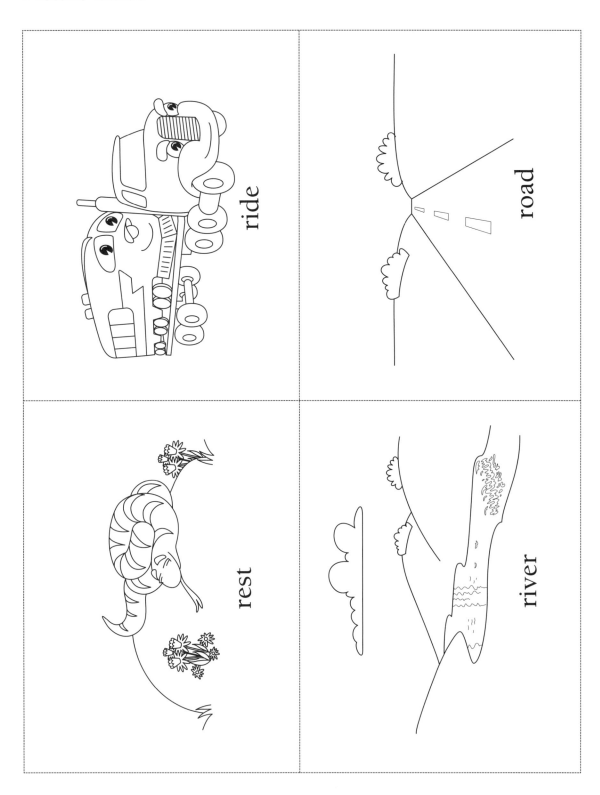

ride

road

rest

river

Picture Cards

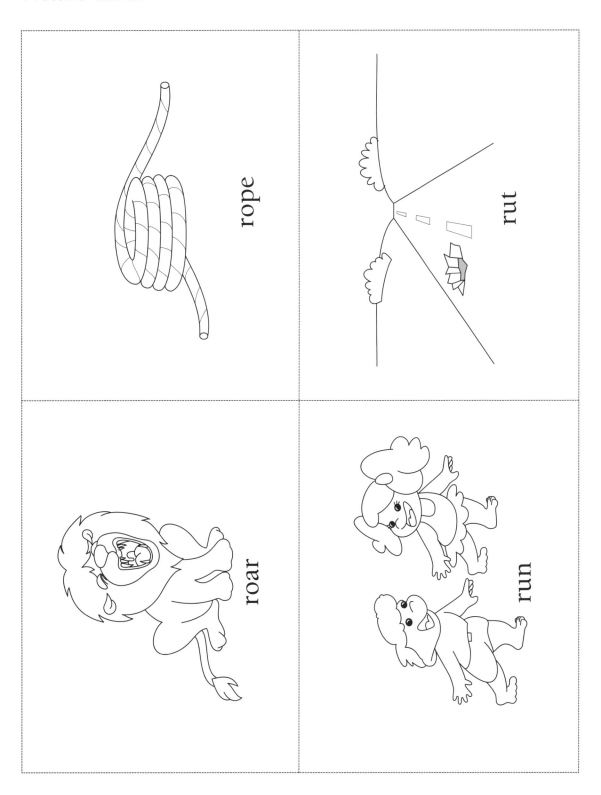

rope

rut

roar

run

Picture Cards

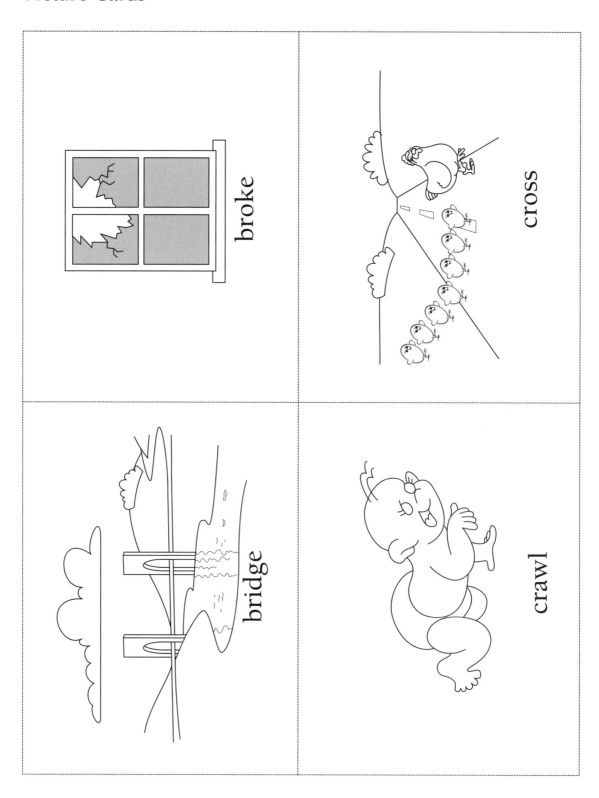

broke

cross

bridge

crawl

Picture Cards

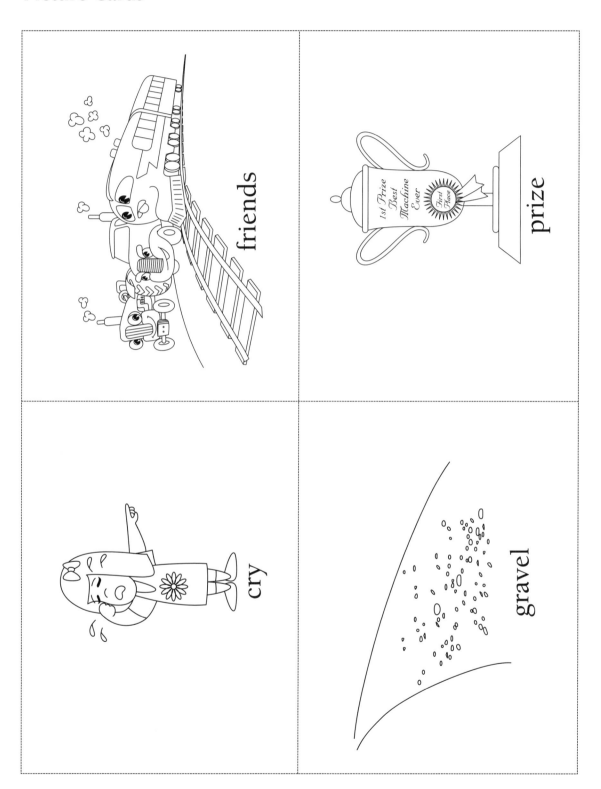

friends

prize

cry

gravel

Picture Cards

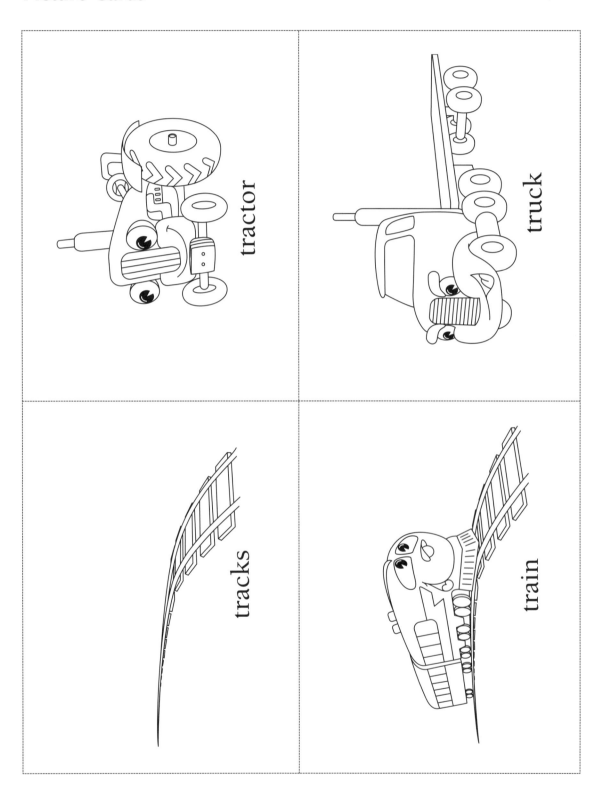

tractor

truck

tracks

train

Word Count Lists

Initial /r/		Initial /r/ Clusters	
Word	Frequency	Word	Frequency
race	2	bragged	1
ran	2	bridge	1
realize	1	broke	1
rest	2	crawl	1
ride	1	creating	1
ridge	1	creek	1
right	2	creeped	1
river	1	cross	1
road	4	crossed	1
roared	1	free	1
		friend	1
		friends	2
		front	1
		gravel	1
		great	1
		ground	1
		group	1
		grumble	1
		pried	1
		prize	3
		problems	1
		three	4
		tracks	1
		tractor	6
		tractor's	2
		tractors	2
		train	10
		trains	2
		traits	1
		trapped	1
		travel	1
		tried	1
		trophy	1
		truck	8
		trucks	2
Total Words: 17		Total Words: 66	

Picture Card Lists

Initial /r/

race
rain
rainbow
read
rest
ride
river
road
roar
rope
run
rut

Initial /r/ Clusters

bridge
broke
crawl
cross
cry
friends
gravel
prize
tracks
tractor
train
truck

Production Practice and Carryover Activities

- Make a **road** or **tracks** with target picture cards. **Drive** toy **trucks**, **tractors**, and **trains** on them. Name the pictures.

- Set up different kinds of races (e.g., **crawling**, **running**, or **riding** bikes).

- Use target picture cards to make a **river** or a **creek**. Take turns **crossing** over the **river**. Name the picture you **cross** over.

- Play London **Bridge**.

- Eat **pretzels** for a snack.

- Glue **pretzels** on a piece of paper to make **train tracks**. **Drive** a toy **train** over the pretzel **tracks**.

- Make an obstacle course with objects that start with /r/. **Ride trikes**, bikes, or scooters around the obstacles. Name the objects.

- Decorate **trophies** or **wrap prizes**. Award them to children for doing their best in **races** or other activities.

- Lay target cards face down in a straight line. Pretend the cards are cars on a **train**. Take turns turning over the cards and telling what is on the **train**.

- Take turns drawing pictures from a container. Use a carrier phrase such as *I walked down the road and I saw*.... Have each person **remember** what has already been said and add his or her picture to the list. Place the pictures face down in a line to make the **road** and see how long your **road** gets before somebody forgets what is there.

Extension Activities

Rhyming

- Do these words rhyme? (yes or no)

race - case	truck - train
rest - best	free - key
road - street	eyes - prize
ride - wide	cross - criss
run - ran	track - back

- Which words rhyme?

tree - free - leaf	truck - duck - train
river - race - base	bridge - ridge - cross
train - try - brain	pry - eye - road
ran - can - brag	rock - gravel - travel
fix - broke - croak	creek - river - beak

- Tell a word that rhymes with *train, road, roar, race, ride, brag, great, track, trap, free.*

Vocabulary Development

- Read the story and discuss vocabulary that may be new to students: *creek, gravel, trophy, claim, traits, ridge, brag, grumble, haul, possess, pry, unique, power to spare, creating a scene, in vain.*

Classification

- Present toy vehicles or pictures of vehicles. Group the vehicles as land, air, or water vehicles.

Comparatives/Superlatives

- Use the story to launch exercises with comparative and superlative adjectives. Use terms such as *faster/fastest* or *stronger/strongest* to describe the vehicles in the story. Introduce the terms *good, better,* and *best.*

Critical Thinking

- Talk about the traits that each of the vehicles possessed in the story. Have children tell which trait they think was the best and why.

- Discuss traits that people have. Have children think of a trait they possess and why it is good to have that trait.

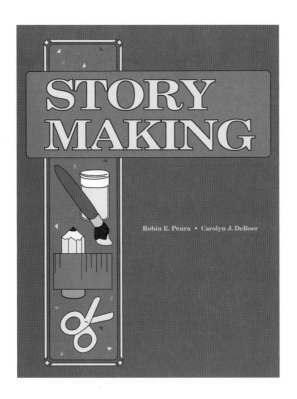